Virtual HR:
Human Resources Management in the Information Age

John W. Jones, Ph.D., ABPP

Virtual HR:
Human Resources Management in the Information Age

John W. Jones, Ph.D., ABPP

CREDITS

Managing Editor: Kathleen Barcos
Editor: Robert Racine
Production: Barbara Atmore
Typesetting: ExecuStaff
Cover Design: FifthStreet Design

Copyright © 1998 by Crisp Publications, Inc.
Printed in the United States of America by Bawden Printing Company.

http://www.crisp-pub.com

Library of Congress Catalog Card Number 97-69692
Jones, John W.
Virtual HR
ISBN 1-56052-473-1

10 9 8 7 6 5 4 3 2 1

This book is printed on recyclable paper with soy ink.

Acknowledgments

I would like to thank Sam Maurice, former President of McGraw-Hill/London House, for supporting this project and for creating an innovative work environment that continuously strives to be on the cutting edge of human resources information technology. I am also grateful to William Terris, Ph.D., for providing me with an opportunity to develop and validate computer-based assessment systems for some of the largest companies in the United States. I also want to thank Mike Lavelli and Doug Ritari for introducing me to the computer revolution.

I am also deeply grateful to three of my colleagues, Joe Orban, Ph.D., Scott Martin, Ph.D., and Wayne Shappard for sharing their ideas and opinions with me about automated human resources assessment systems. I owe a special thanks to Jim Turner for inviting me to present my early thoughts on this subject at an annual meeting of Chicago-area human resource executives. I also would like to thank Lisa Griegel, Gladys Hawkins, and Verona Haffenden for preparing countless versions of this manuscript.

As always, I am deeply grateful to my wife, Kati Soto Jones, and my children, Alexander and William Jones, for all of their support during the writing of this book. Finally, I dedicate this book to my grandmother, Ella Pusey, who passed away before this book was completed. My grandmother has always been a scholar who enriched the lives of all her family members through her hard work and commitment to higher education. I am thankful that I had an opportunity to adopt her value system and work ethic.

John W. Jones, Ph.D., ABPP

Industrial-Organizational Psychologist

Contents

WITHDRAWN

PART 1

Virtual HR: An Overview

CHAPTER 1

Virtual HR: The Paradigm Shift

VIRTUAL HR DEFINED

Organizational futurists were the first to conceptualize a wide variety of "virtual" cultures. Well-known examples include the virtual university, the virtual office, and even the virtual workplace. For instance, a virtual workplace has been defined as an organization where employees can work from remote sites (e.g., home offices, client sites, and hotels) by being electronically connected to their company's business and communication systems.

Three of the most widely accepted definitions of the word "virtual" include: (1) a condition without boundaries or constraints; (2) something without a physical presence that is not quite what it appears to be; and, more specifically, (3) the use of computer hardware, software, and networks to carry out a wide variety of business functions. The first definition is relevant to virtual universities. The second definition is relevant to virtual corporations whose "storefront" is a web site in cyberspace. The third definition is relevant to telecommuters who work out of their virtual home office. All three definitions are consistent with the theme of relying on information technology to do more with less.

"Virtual HR" is typically defined as the use of computer systems, interactive electronic media, and telecommunication networks to carry out the functions of the human resources department. Virtual HR managers always strive to provide a seamless integration of all HR services with a common goal of employee satisfaction. This technology-assisted model of HR is often begun as an efficiency program, but it soon evolves into a major source of competitive advantage. In addition, while some human resources departments utilize a few virtual HR applications, others strive to reengineer, automate, and integrate nearly all of their HR functions. Virtual HR lowers costs and improves efficiencies by:

◆ Reducing paperwork and streamlining work flow

◆ Automating redundant HR tasks

◆ Empowering employees to embrace a self-service HR delivery system

◆ Keeping the company's workforce fully informed about all important HR compliance issues and corporate events

◆ Speeding up the response time of HR systems

◆ Ensuring that more informed decisions are made

◆ Improving time management

◆ Offering a flexible model of HR that meets the changing needs of an increasingly diverse and global workforce

THE DRIVING FORCES OF CHANGE

There is a paradigm shift occurring in HR departments toward the strategic management of HR information through the innovative application of information technology. This shift relies less on a large staff to administrate the HR department and more on information technology (e.g., client–server networks) to form the backbone of an information-rich, self-service model of human resource management. History has shown that the most successful companies always keep pace with such paradigm shifts.

The evolution of the virtual HR department is based on six driving forces. These forces need to be harnessed and responded to as companies approach the 21st century. The following six forces must be addressed by HR departments that want to continuously increase their value while reducing costs.

1. *Information Technology.* HR professionals are facing a digital future. The rapid growth in the field of computer hardware, software, networking, and telephony services is absolutely essential to the virtual HR movement. It is no accident that virtual HR departments will become the norm in the near future. This is especially true with the increased sophistication and lower costs of Information Age technology and automated processes.

2. *Process Reengineering.* Strategic HR managers are constantly looking for ways to streamline and improve core business processes to make them more efficient. All business processes, especially those in the HR department, can be reengineered and improved through the skillful application of information technology.

3. *High-Speed Management.* To be competitive, all companies must work smarter and faster. Virtual HR is definitely a smarter and quicker form of service delivery than traditional HR.

4. *Networked Organizations.* Virtual HR departments are more likely to emerge in networked organizations than in traditional and bureaucratic companies. Companies are delayering and restructuring in an effort to become less bureaucratic and more efficient. The proliferation of information technology such as local area networks, e-mail, and corporate Intranets are the trademarks of a flatter, networked company. These new-wave organizations offer state-of-the-art technology and information sharing to empower all levels of personnel.

5. *Knowledge Workers.* The 21st-century organization will compete on strategic information and knowledge. These "learning organizations" will be staffed with self-directed, and computer-savvy, knowledge workers. These workers will excel at using information to quickly identify and capture lucrative business opportunities, while also diligently identifying and resolving costly problems. Virtual HR managers have no choice but to empower these knowledge workers with real-time HR information and just-in-time computer-assisted learning experiences.

6. *Globalization.* To compete successfully in the 21st century, nearly all companies must develop a global business strategy. This means that HR departments must be capable of servicing their employees anywhere on Earth. Obviously, a technology-assisted HR department that is skilled at traversing the information superhighway is in the best position to support a globalized workforce.

In summary, all of the aforementioned forces are designed to get rid of outmoded organizational processes, procedures, layers, and boundaries that add cost and form barriers between the human resources department and the company employees. Moreover, all of these forces reflect the enormous impact that information technology is having, and will continue to have, on every process and procedure in the HR department. The successful implementation of a virtual HR department will clearly increase a company's competitive advantage.

CORE VIRTUAL HR TECHNOLOGIES

This book is not designed to teach HR professionals everything about all of the emerging HR information management technologies. However, Appendix A includes a fairly comprehensive listing of the most important computer-related terms and concepts that must be mastered by all aspiring virtual HR professionals. In addition, some of the more important core technologies that provide the foundation for the virtual HR movement are summarized below. Virtual HR professionals should at least know the rudiments of: **(1)** powerful central processing unit technologies, **(2)** client–server technologies, **(3)** computer telephony integration technologies, **(4)** Internet/Intranet technologies, and **(5)** network architecture and design.

1. **Powerful Central Processing Unit Technologies**: The central processing unit (CPU) is the actual "brains" or calculating part of the computer. The CPU processes instructions, performs calculations, and manages information flow through the computer. The virtual HR movement is being fueled in large part by the evolution of very powerful CPU's. Newer, more powerful CPU's, such as Intel's new MMX Pentium and Pentium II processors, are able to perform significantly more instructions at one time while also computing at considerably faster speeds. Intel's MMX processor line is especially relevant to interactive multimedia, improving the performance of such tasks as processing of graphics, video, and sound. Finally, other CPU extensions, such as math co-processors, allow Virtual HR professionals to excel at HR data warehousing, mining, and statistical analysis.

2. **Client–Server Technologies**: Client–server architecture exists when a "client" computer is the requesting machine and the information "server" is the machine supplying data. The employees' computers are the "clients" or requesting machines. Clients provide the user interface and perform the bulk of the applications processing. The HR department's computers are the "servers" or supplying machines. Servers can be high-speed microcomputers, minicomputers, or even mainframes. For example, a database server maintains the HR databases and processes requests from

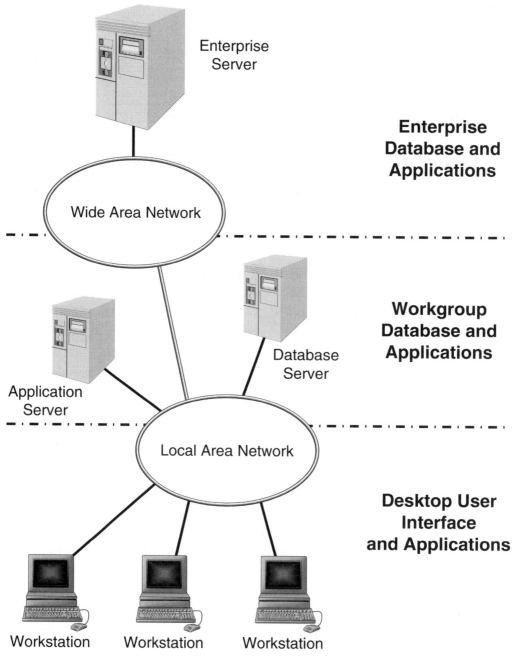

Enterprise
Server

**Enterprise
Database and
Applications**

Wide Area Network

**Workgroup
Database and
Applications**

Database
Server

Application
Server

Local Area Network

**Desktop User
Interface
and Applications**

Workstation   Workstation   Workstation

Multi-level Network Design

employees to extract data from or update the database. This is a very important capability in the self-service model of virtual HR. An application server provides additional business processing capabilties, such as the ability to scan in and analyze resumes, and even computer administer, score, and interpret personnel tests and surveys.

Client–server networks are a highly efficient way to connect a large number of computers exchanging large amounts of information. The client–server architecture makes information and computing power available where work is performed. Moreover, the hardware, software, and other operational costs are lower than those for mainframe systems.

3. **Computer Telephony Integration Technologies:** This category of virtual HR technologies deals with the integration of computers and telephones. Basic computer telephony messaging applications include voice mail, fax blasters, unified messaging, and fax on demand. This group of technologies also ensures that employees are electronically connected through autoattendants, audio- and videoconferencing, one-number universal services, smart card services, value-added services for both wireless and landline phones, and call-center enhancements. Finally, computer telephony technologies provide employees with unique formats for responding and interacting over the phone, such as HR database access through the phone and interactive voice response (IVR) systems. These IVR systems release HR staff from an overwhelming number of routine transaction calls, while also enabling 24-hour self-service. It must be noted that specialists in computer telephony are also working on integrating the Internet into their computer telephony solutions. Yet as described below, the Internet is a stand-alone core virtual HR technology.

4. **Internet/Intranet Technologies:** A key set of virtual HR technologies relates to the Internet. The Internet is oftentimes referred to as the world's largest computer network used by tens of millions of people. The Internet is made possible by a set of communication protocols (e.g., transmission control protocal/Internet protocal [TCP/IP]) that allow for the

internetworking of dissimilar systems. The Internet is not an on-line service and has no central "hub." Rather, it is a large network made up of thousands of smaller interconnected networks.

The World Wide Web is part of the Internet and consists of a very large collection of documents stored on computers around the world. Web browsers are another core Internet/Intranet technology. Web browsers are programs that allow employees to view and explore information on the Web. Browsers such as the Netscape Navigator and the Microsoft Internet Explorer allow users to download World Wide Web pages and immediately view them on their computers. Browsers rely on the Internet's standardized addressing system of Universal Resource Locators (URLs) to locate relevant Web pages. These Web pages are created using hypertext markup language, or HTML. These hypertext documents contain highlighted or tagged text that connects to other pages on the Web. Users can easily jump from one Web page to the next by selecting the highlighted text. More amazingly, selecting highlighted text can take you to a Web page on the same computer or a computer on the other side of the world!

Thousands of companies have private Web sites, or Intranets, where employees can obtain company information, manage their benefits plan, and even apply for a new job. These Intranets are private company networks that are based on the exact same technologies (i.e., browsers, Web pages, HTML) as the World Wide Web. Needless to say, virtual HR professionals rely heavily on both Internet and Intranet technologies. All of the major on-line service providers (e.g., America On-line, CompuServe, the Microsoft Network) offer access to the Internet.

5. **Network Architecture and Design:** Virtual HR professionals must help in the design of their virtual HR systems. These systems should be designed to: (1) rapidly distribute critical HR data and services, (2) dramatically reduce the number of steps in their HR applications, and (3) provide new HR services and strategic uses of HR information. The network architecture determines future flexibility and scalability, and involves the design and maintenance of the entire virtual HR computer

network, including hardware, software, access methods, and protocols. For example, the technology infrastructure can be broken down into: (1) user interface functions (e.g., all data input and output methods and processes), (2) application functions (e.g., the software programs that do the work), (3) data access functions (e.g., interface routines, database management systems, editing programs), (4) distributed services (e.g., HR databases), and (5) client workstations or network computers, to name a few. A properly designed and implemented architecture facilitates employee collaboration, ensures highly efficient network applications, and is the essential step in building a highly integrated virtual HR infrastructure.

HR MANAGEMENT MEGATRENDS

TRADITIONAL HR	VIRTUAL HR
1. Paper-intensive job.	1. Paperless office environment.
2. People skills dominate.	2. Information management and technology mastery skills are essential.
3. Data filing and information dissemination are key functions.	3. Strategic HR management skills and systems-level thinking are critical.
4. The HR department is functionally oriented.	4. The virtual HR staff assume more of a consultative/advisory role.
5. Less scientific sources of personnel information are relied on (e.g., traditional interviews).	5. More scientific sources of HR information are used (e.g., computer-based personnel testing).
6. HR professionals react to new information technologies (IT) recommended by their IT departments.	6. Technology-savvy virtual HR professionals proactively request cutting-edge technologies from their IT group.

THE EMERGENCE OF VIRTUAL HR

Watson-Wyatt, a technology-oriented HR consulting firm, is a leading researcher of the virtual HR movement. Watson-Wyatt oftentimes posts its groundbreaking research on the World Wide Web (see URL: http://www.watsonwyatt.com). Watson-Wyatt researchers recently conducted a study in which they asked 343 companies in 10 industries about their use of virtual HR applications. The firm's key findings are summarized below.

Major Findings

1. The movement toward virtual HR has been progressing at a rapid pace for more than a decade. One major goal fueling this movement is to free the HR department from excessive administrative demands so that it may serve a more strategic role within its company. Another major goal is to increase a company's competitiveness.

2. Watson-Wyatt found that, by 1997, 53% of companies used interactive voice response (IVR) systems for HR purposes, and this figure is expected to grow to 78% within two years. Similarly, 32% currently use multimedia computers and 22% use interactive kiosks for HR applications. These figures should increase to 52% and 59%, respectively, within the next two years. Moreover, approximately 27% of respondents implemented a Web-based virtual HR application and a full 64% plan to implement one within the next year! These Watson-Wyatt figures support the vision of becoming a strategically centered, self-service HR department.

3. The Watson-Wyatt study also identified some of the current leading Web-based HR applications: (a) job postings and recruitment (70%), (b) corporate communications (57%), (c) benefits information and enrollment (32%), (d) on-line training (24%), (e) access to profit sharing, savings, and 401(k) services (18%), and (f) on-line performance appraisal and

management services (6%). All other Web-based virtual HR applications (e.g., collaboration via Groupware, personnel interviewing systems) yielded a 19% response rate. In addition, supplemental survey questions revealed that all of these percentages would increase dramatically within the next few years.

4. Watson-Wyatt researchers also asked respondents to share their primary reasons for implementing virtual HR technology. Their main reasons, in order, were: (a) improved service to employees (33%), (b) enhanced communications with employees (24%), (c) cost reductions (9%), (d) productivity increases (9%), (e) reduced HR staffing requirements (3%), and (f) improved transaction accuracy (3%). Nineteen percent said they either did not have a primary reason (6%) or there was another, more esoteric reason (13%). Watson-Wyatt researchers interpreted these findings to mean that virtual HR is primarily a tool for achieving strategic goals, although it also reduces costs.

5. This study also examined the costs and resources required to implement *basic* Web-based Intranet technology. Basic applications include the provision of on-line HR documentation and job postings, along with one-way communications. Forty-three percent of respondents reported that their total costs for developing and implementing their streamlined Web-based application was under $50,000. Sixteen percent said the total cost was $50,000 to $100,000, and 13% reported that the total cost was over $100,000. Approximately 28% did not know. In addition, approximately 49% of respondents used only internal staff to develop their virtual HR applications, 2% used only external staff, and a full 44% used some combination of these. Yet this last group forecasted that for future application development, only 23% would rely on internal staff only, 3% would rely on external staff only, and a full 65% would rely on some combination of these resources. The clear trend seems to be to partner with external development experts.

6. Finally, the Watson-Wyatt survey revealed how useful the respondents' employees found the virtual HR applications to be. Approximately 66% reported that their employees found the applications to be "useful" (Very Useful = 28%; Somewhat Useful = 38%). These respondents also felt that the virtual HR applications successfully met their strategic objectives. Approximately 6% reported that their employees did not find the applications useful, and 28% did not yet survey their employees' perceptions of and experiences with the new virtual HR technologies. Virtual HR professionals must always seek feedback from their end users.

CHAPTER 2

Technology-Enabled Human Resources

REENGINEERING HR

The virtual HR movement is usually implemented as part of a corporate reengineering initiative. Hence, aspiring virtual HR professionals must be knowledgeable about business process reengineering. "Reengineering" is typically defined as the fundamental rethinking and radical redesign of human resource processes to bring about dramatic improvements in overall service quality while also reducing costs. That is, HR reengineering requires one to look at the fundamental HR processes from a technology-assisted perspective. There are four key words in the aforementioned definition that must be thoroughly understood by aspiring virtual HR professionals.

◆ *Radical*—Virtual HR managers must be willing to start over with a clean slate. Instead of just settling for a slight improvement in quality, such managers must boldly think in terms of grand reengineering strategies.

◆ *Redesign*—Virtual HR managers must creatively conceptualize and design new HR processes. These managers must embrace quality improvement goals like Faster, Cheaper, and Better. Instead of simply fitting technology to old HR processes and procedures that should have been eliminated, virtual HR managers need to think of totally new ways of providing HR services with the help of enabling information technologies.

◆ *Processes*—An HR process is a group of related tasks that create value for employees, managers, and, ultimately, the corporate shareholders. Aspiring virtual HR managers must target those HR processes that bring true value to the corporation. They then need to reengineer those mission-critical processes so that they bring even greater value at a lower cost through the use of cutting-edge information management technology.

◆ *Dramatic*—Finally, virtual HR managers must always make a quantum leap in performance. One should not squander valuable corporate resources on marginal HR reengineering projects. In addition, adopting new virtual HR applications should lead to a documented improvement in both the quality of employees and the competitive posture of the company. Ideally, these gains will be based on a lower cost structure and enhanced organizational performance.

Ten Factors for Successful Reengineering

Research has identified 10 factors that should ensure the successful reengineering of a traditional HR department into a virtual HR department. These factors should be fully embraced by all aspiring virtual HR managers.

1. *Automate the core HR processes.* What are the mission critical processes in your HR department that should be reengineered first?

_____

_____

_____

2. *Quickly diagnose the current situation.* Virtual HR managers do not let grass grow under their feet. They are "high-speed" managers when it comes to transforming their HR departments from a traditional to a contemporary model. What can you immediately do to speed up the implementation or further development of a virtual HR department at your company?

_____

_____

_____

3. *Ensure strong, multilevel leadership.* Virtual HR managers seek full support for their projects from both senior executives and key decision makers in various end-user groups. Who could you select to head up the virtual HR transformation team at your company? Who are some critically important potential team members?

_____

_____

_____

4. *Seek radical, breakthrough ideas.* Virtual HR managers are looking for quantum leaps in their reengineering efforts. Therefore, creative ideas and solutions must address a wide variety of questions (e.g., Which HR processes should be reengineered first? Should we build or buy technology-enabled HR applications? What corporate obstacles could impede our progress?). What are some effective strategies for soliciting breakthrough ideas and solutions with this type of HR reengineering project?

_____

_____

_____

5. *Consider the entire HR department.* Aspiring virtual HR managers need to consider reengineering all HR processes and applications that fall under the responsibility of the HR department. There should be no "sacred cows." Are there certain HR processes and applications that might be easily overlooked in your virtual HR reengineering efforts?

_____

_____

_____

6. *Reengineering quickly.* Once the traditional HR processes are mapped out and prioritized, and once a multilevel and interdepartmental reengineering team is established and has received funding, then the transformation process should begin. Project plans and production schedules should be developed that ensure "speed to market" at a

reasonable cost. What type of automated planning, scheduling, and resource allocation software would you use with this type of project?

_____

_____

_____

7. *Test out a "laboratory" version.* Virtual HR managers never implement a technology-enabled application without thoroughly testing all of the application's features and functions. How can you ensure that your virtual HR applications and integrated systems are thoroughly tested and approved before they are officially released?

_____

_____

_____

8. *Ensure that end users are satisfied.* Usability studies are needed to make sure that all employees are fully satisfied with the new virtual HR systems. All virtual HR systems should be user-friendly and should provide documented value to all levels of employees. What methodologies can you use to monitor end-user satisfaction?

_____

_____

_____

9. *Adopt an entrepreneurial implementation style.* Virtual HR managers never naively assume that their employees and managers will automatically flock to the new virtual HR systems. Instead, such managers rely on internal marketing promotions and contests to ensure that all employees and managers frequently utilize the reengineered and automated HR systems. What internal marketing strategies could you use to make sure that all levels of employees embrace your virtual HR systems?

_____

_____

_____

10. *Attend to the ever-changing needs of end users.* Finally, once a traditional HR process is automated into a virtual HR process, the manager must remain committed to constantly upgrading and improving the new technology-enabled HR process. This ensures that the very best HR content will always be utilized on the most cutting-edge technology systems. Such a commitment should ensure ongoing support of the virtual HR movement. How do you plan to objectively assess your end users' HR needs on a continuing basis?

_____

_____

_____

HR INFORMATION AND TECHNOLOGY: THE INTERFACE

The future of virtual HR departments revolves around the integration of technology with strategically-oriented HR information in order to add value to the company. Technology can be either burdensome or enabling. Burdensome technology is typically characterized as outdated, underutilized, or simply poor performing. Enabling technology is fast, efficient, and user-friendly. In addition to utilizing enabling technology, effective information management is a core activity of nearly all virtual HR departments. Any virtual HR program would be seriously flawed if the major focus was on automating paperwork without challenging the quality of the HR data. Therefore, to add real economic value to the company, HR professionals must also collect and utilize accurate, relevant, and scientifically sound HR data. In reality, the information collected by most HR professionals actually ranges from being inaccurate and invalid (e.g., from a poorly executed performance appraisal or job interview) to being valid and reliable (e.g., from a scientifically-based organizational survey). Needless to say, virtual HR professionals always strive to utilize user-friendly and enabling technologies that potentiate highly valid and reliable HR information. See the following figure and assess which cell your HR department falls into.

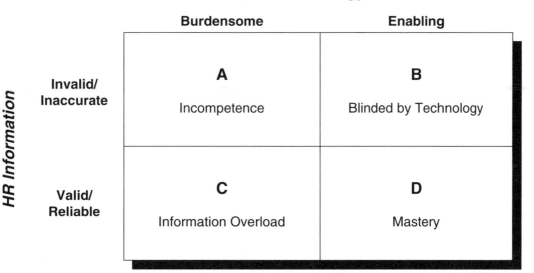

Cell Profiles

A. *Incompetence*

The worst situation occurs when the technology is burdensome and the information you have is invalid or inaccurate. In such a case, there is little commitment to cutting-edge technology, and the integrity of the HR information databases and assessment results is highly suspect. While an abundance of HR information is probably being collected and used, the scientific accuracy of the information is extremely suspect (e.g., performance appraisals are conducted by supervisors who were not trained to rate their employees accurately; only subjective and prejudicial employment interviews were conducted; the database of critical personnel information [e.g., benefits enrollment] is not updated and quality-checked on a regular basis).

B. *Blinded by Technology*

A deceptive situation occurs when you are enabled by the technology but the information remains invalid or inaccurate. Even though the HR department has access to the very best in enabling technology, the quality of its information is still suspect. What is extremely deceptive about this cell is that HR professionals can easily become seduced by the technology without questioning the validity and reliability of their databases and information sources. Obviously, the quality of all information-based business decisions will suffer in this situation.

C. *Information Overload*

The good news in this situation is that accurate HR databases are established, maintained, and utilized. Only the most scientific information-gathering tools are utilized (e.g., valid and reliable personnel testing programs for new hires instead of subjective and prejudicial interviews; succession planning lists developed from extremely accurate performance reviews and career development plans). The major limitation of this cell is that reliance on burdensome technology does not ease any of the information management demands. This can only lead to heightened job stress and burnout among HR professionals.

D. *Mastery*

This is the home of the virtual HR superstars! Enabling technologies such as HR Intranets, multimedia training modules, and computerized personnel assessment systems are routinely utilized. Moreover, high-quality HR databases are always established, maintained, and mined to ensure a strong competitive advantage. In addition, virtual HR professionals always avoid information overload and technostress due to their reliance on sound information-gathering and technology management principles.

VIRTUAL HR SYSTEM DEVELOPMENT

Virtual HR professionals face a number of important strategic decisions. One is the "buy versus build" dilemma. If a core competency within an HR professional's company is related to software development and the strategic management of information, then the company might choose to build the technology infrastructure to support a virtual HR initiative. However, if these resources are unavailable or nonexistent, then the development must be outsourced. In addition, virtual HR professionals must decide whether they want to manage a virtual HR application internally (e.g., an electronic recruitment system) or whether they want to outsource the entire management function to a company that specializes in a particular application (e.g., a payroll and benefits management provider). Finally, virtual HR professionals need to make these strategic decisions in relation to both stand-alone applications (e.g., computerized testing) and advanced integrated systems (e.g., human resource information systems). All of these issues are summarized on the following page.

LEADING VIRTUAL HR APPLICATIONS

It is beyond the scope of this text to provide an exhaustive list of all available virtual HR applications. However, the following list is a summary of the most common applications advertised in leading trade magazines and product catalogs. Place a check mark next to all the systems that you are currently

Virtual HR System Development

	Internal	External
	Virtual HR Is Core Competency	**Rapid Implementation Is Goal**
Internal	◆ Company has skills to develop and implement virtual HR technology. ◆ Company requires a very customized system that it wants to control completely. ◆ Highest fixed-cost structure.	◆ System development is quicker from outside vendors. ◆ Off-the-shelf systems or quasi-customized systems are very acceptable for reaching the company's goals. ◆ Company wants to retain full control of sensitive corporate databases.
	Greater Service at Lower Cost	**Full Outsourcing of Virtual HR**
External	◆ System management is not the company's core competency. ◆ Vendor provides greater support and service at lower cost. ◆ Temporary workers can help manage the system.	◆ HR prefers to focus on strategy building and not system development and maintenance. ◆ Outsourcing reduces fixed costs associated with building and maintaining the system. ◆ The vendor must be a credible long-term partner who shares the virtual HR manager's vision.

HR System Management

knowledgeable about or that you have actually tested or implemented. Parenthetically, this text will focus on the more dominant virtual HR applications, including HR Intranets, on-line recruitment services, computerized assessments, and technology-assisted training, to name a few.

Leading Virtual HR Applications (Partial Listing)	Knowledgeable About	Have Tested or Implemented
1. CD-ROM collection of HR regulations	❏	❏
2. On-line job analysis and job description system	❏	❏
3. On-line virtual recruitment centers (both interactive voice response systems and Web-based services)	❏	❏
4. Computerized interviews and background checks	❏	❏
5. Computer-based personnel tests	❏	❏
6. Computer-based training	❏	❏
7. Interactive multimedia training	❏	❏
8. Web-based training	❏	❏
9. Virtual reality training	❏	❏
10. Training management software	❏	❏

11. HR Intranets and Groupware ❑ ❑

12. Human resource information systems ❑ ❑

13. HR data warehousing, mining, and statistical analysis software ❑ ❑

14. Performance appraisal software ❑ ❑

15. Personnel policies development software ❑ ❑

16. Personnel scheduling and tracking software ❑ ❑

17. On-line employment law resources ❑ ❑

18. Payroll and benefits management applications ❑ ❑

19. Organizational survey design and administration software ❑ ❑

20. Strategic HR research on the Web ❑ ❑

What other virtual HR applications and services have you been exposed to?

_____

_____

_____

_____

COST-JUSTIFYING VIRTUAL HR

Virtual HR professionals need to cost-justify their investments. That is, reengineering a human resource program should always be a bottom-line business decision. While virtual HR professionals are encouraged to use sophisticated return-on-investment formulas (e.g., internal rate of return, net present value), the upcoming worksheet can be used to obtain a quick yet reasonable "ballpark" estimate.

The early approaches to cost-justifying virtual HR systems and applications focused almost exclusively on expense reduction. Quite simply, the accountant focused on the HR administration costs that were eliminated after virtual HR applications were implemented. Yet virtual HR programs can be cost-justified in more ways than just administrative savings. For example, virtual HR delivers a broad range of strategic information services that allow an organization to be very competitive by improving: (1) workforce utilization, (2) organizational development, (3) performance outcomes, and (4) corporate adaptation and flexibility, to name a few. Therefore, virtual HR managers should always take credit when their computer-assisted HR programs help the organization perform better or reach its business objectives quicker.

The upcoming worksheet for estimating total return on investment (ROI) is based on a timely article by Minneman (1996). Minneman cataloged most of the cost elements related to a comprehensive virtual HR program including application software, hardware, architectural software, telecommunications, and implementation.

The key challenge with the worksheet is the estimation of the Value-Added column, which should include the dollar amount saved through expense reduction, along with the estimated dollar value obtained when a virtual HR application helps an organization reach its productivity, quality, and service objectives.

In each section of the worksheet, consider all costs and benefits related to a particular virtual HR element line. For example, to estimate the costs and the value-added return for both a computerized preemployment testing program and an interactive multimedia training module, a virtual HR professional would come up with the following estimates for the Niche Applications row found in Section I: Application Software.

	Preemployment Testing	Multimedia Training	Total Niche Applications
Development Costs	$125,000	$75,000	$200,000
Operation Costs			
Year 1	$45,000	$55,000	$100,000
Year 2	$35,000	$45,000	$80,000
Total Development	$205,000	$175,000	$380,000
Value-Added Return			
Administrative Cost Reduction:			
Year 1	$100,000	$95,000	$195,000
Year 2	$120,000	$85,000	$205,000
Strategic Contributions: (Increased Productivity, Improved Quality, and Stronger Customer Service)			
Year 1	$450,000	$350,000	$800,000
Year 2	$550,000	$400,000	$950,000
Total Value Added	$1,220,000	$930,000	$2,150,000

$$\text{Value-Added ROI} = \frac{(\text{Total Value Added} - \text{Total Costs})}{\text{Total Costs}}$$

$$= \frac{(\$2,150,000 - \$380,000)}{\$380,000}$$

$$= 4.66 \text{ to } 1, \text{ or } 466\% \text{ Return}$$

To use the following worksheet to assess the total return on investment (ROI) for a comprehensive virtual HR program, simply estimate the development and operation costs along with the value-added return (i.e., cost reductions and performance enhancement) for all of the cost elements. This would allow virtual HR professionals to come up with a wide variety of ROI outcomes, including:

◆ Overall two-year ROI

◆ Overall Year 1 and Year 2 ROIs

◆ Overall ROIs for each of the five cost categories

◆ Year 1 and Year 2 ROIs for each of the cost categories

Estimating Total ROI

Virtual HR Program Elements	Development Costs	Operation Costs		Value Added	
		Yr. 1	Yr. 2	Yr. 1	Yr. 2
I. Application Software					
• Core Human Resource Information System Programs	____	____	____	____	____
• Niche Applications	____	____	____	____	____
• Enabling Applications	____	____	____	____	____
II. Hardware					
• Dedicated Servers	____	____	____	____	____
• Client Workstations (new and upgraded)	____	____	____	____	____
• Other Hardware	____	____	____	____	____

Virtual HR Program Elements	Development Costs	Operation Costs		Value Added	
		Yr. 1	Yr. 2	Yr. 1	Yr. 2
III. Architectural Software					
• Operating Systems	____	____	____	____	____
• Database Management Systems	____	____	____	____	____
• Data Access Tools	____	____	____	____	____
• Statistical Analysis Programs	____	____	____	____	____
• Other Software Fees (licensing and development)	____	____	____	____	____
IV. Telecommunications					
• Local Area Networks	____	____	____	____	____
• Wide Area Networks	____	____	____	____	____
• Internet Usage Fees	____	____	____	____	____
• Miscellaneous Telephony Costs	____	____	____	____	____
V. Implementation					
• Internal Business Resources	____	____	____	____	____
• External Consultants	____	____	____	____	____
• Project Teams	____	____	____	____	____
• Other Reengineering Costs	____	____	____	____	____
• Other Information	____	____	____	____	____
• Technology Costs	____	____	____	____	____
Totals	____	____	____	____	____

DOCUMENTING THE IMPACT OF VIRTUAL HR

Case studies that document the impact of Virtual HR programs have recently been published. A representative sample of these studies is provided below. Additional case studies are provided throughout this text.

◆ Price Waterhouse, an audit, tax accounting, and business consulting company, used a multimedia training program to train 7,000 auditors in 50 countries. Price Waterhouse found that this computer-based training program reduced learning time by 50% compared with traditional training. A return-on-investment analysis revealed that the total cost per learner for the virtual HR method was $106 versus $760 for the traditional training method (Hall, 1996).

◆ Osram-Sylvania is a producer of lighting products. This company used the groupware features in the Web-enabled version of Lotus Notes to automate the company's benefits administration and job-posting processes. Employees now handle all record updates without any assistance from HR. The real-time recruiting process reduced the hiring time from weeks to days. In addition, program evaluation research revealed the following: (a) employees are satisfied with the virtual HR system, (b) the system is saving $130,000 a year on data collection services alone, and (c) the number of applicants for posted jobs has increased by 33% (Greengard, 1997).

◆ Videoconferencing systems are finally coming of age. In 1996, approximately 300,000 business desktop systems and 25,000 room systems were shipped. Success stories are also starting to surface. For instance, Ralph Ungermann, CEO of First Virtual Corporation, reported that he did not take a business trip for seven months thanks to videoconferencing. This led to considerable expense reduction (McNamara, 1997).

◆ Corporations are leaping headfirst into Intranet waters. Most of these early adopters do not even care about return-on-investment (ROI) studies. These early adopters point out that few ROI studies were conducted when companies moved from electronic typewriters to computerized word processors. Still, a consultancy company called Cadence Design Systems, of San Jose, California, used Intranet technology to reduce its sales cycle. That is, this company developed an Intranet that allowed new sales representatives to quickly access information that would teach them about the 1,000 plus items in their product line. These sales representatives also used the Intranet to access customer information databases to better understand their buying needs. On-line sales training modules also thoroughly mapped out and described each phase of the sales process. The Intranet along with the sales training modules had a three-year cost of approximately $1.4 million, yet within a few months the return from training covered this expense. In fact, Cadence documented a 1,700% return on their Intranet-based sales training program (Korzeniowski, 1997).

PART 2

Applications and Integrated Systems

CHAPTER 3

HR Intranets: A Self-Service Revolution

OVERVIEW

Companies are migrating away from a centralized human resources management system and toward HR Intranets that are complemented by client–server technologies (Shadovitz, 1996). HR Intranets enable virtual HR professionals to employ the same types of servers and browsers used with the World Wide Web for internal applications over their corporate networks. Intranets provide a way for an HR department to enhance its service offerings to employees while also improving communication, efficiency, and productivity within the corporation. For example, HR Intranets allow human resources departments to be open virtually 24 hours a day, 365 days per year. Most important, this unlimited access requires minimal effort from the HR staff.

The Intranet can increase HR's contribution to both strategic and financial goals. Some of the major benefits derived from Intranets are listed next.

◆ An ideal platform for continuously updating internal HR policies, procedures, and other publications.

◆ A powerful, yet inexpensive communications system that can provide information anywhere at anytime.

◆ Intranet technology can be used across wide area networks.

◆ Web servers do not need large capital expenditures in hardware, and Web server software interoperates well.

◆ Web browsers are compatible with most platforms.

◆ Interoperability and flexibility allows Intranets to send information directly to the employees' remote printers, e-mail accounts, fax machines, and videoconferencing systems.

◆ Since most employees are familiar with Web browsing tools, a corporation can avoid the costly training and support that comes with more complex Groupware programs.

Most of the routine HR tasks can be conducted over the Intranet. The HR Intranet makes information available for internal use, while eliminating the printing and distribution costs of employee handbooks and manuals. The Intranet also minimizes the use of outdated HR information since it is easy to edit and update information on a single database server. The Intranet allows for the rapid dissemination of important information on a wide variety of HR topics, including, but not limited to:

◆ Company mission and goals

◆ The employee handbook and policies

◆ Help-desk and technical support

◆ A compensation manual

◆ Employee benefits information and on-line enrollment

◆ Occupational health and safety information

◆ Job postings and transfer procedures

◆ Employee training and development resources

◆ Searchable telephone directories

◆ In-house newsletters or publications

◆ Company announcements

◆ Group and team communications

◆ Departmental and employee home pages

◆ Product and company information

◆ Corporate research summaries

◆ Commuting and child care options

◆ Posting of new employment laws

◆ Training and videoconferencing

◆ Internet E-mail and voice mail

The HR Intranet is also a self-service network that facilitates the collection of information from employees. That is, most Intranets also include a variety of

HR forms that can be completed on-line. This reduces paperwork and helps to optimize the efficiency of the HR department. Examples of secure Intranet applications, where access is restricted to other departments and employees, include:

◆ Employee enrollment in benefit plans (e.g., 401K programs)

◆ Reports of change in employee status

◆ Employee surveys and feedback questionnaires

◆ Confidential employee review of employee accounts, such as vacation balances, investment options, and sick day usage.

In summary, HR Intranets are a more dynamic way of linking employees to HR information that is immediate, cost effective, and easy to use. Most important, they enable employees to perform a wide variety of HR-related tasks with minimal involvement from the HR department.

EMPLOYEE SELF-SERVICE

A key goal of virtual HR is to facilitate employee self-service programs. The self-service paradigm allows employees to find answers to their own HR questions. Employees can also access and revise/update their own personnel data. In addition, employees can complete required HR forms on-line, as well as execute a number of important transactions (e.g., setting their investment allocations in the company's profit-sharing plan).

Traditionally, the HR department interacted with employees directly and provided a high level of individual attention. These types of HR communications have historically been paper-based. Yet current business demands (e.g., downsizing, rightsizing, and smartsizing) are requiring HR professionals to do more with less, despite the fact that HR issues are becoming more complex. Employees also have more questions to ask. Therefore, it is essential that

HR professionals create technology-enabled self-service systems (e.g., HR Intranets) that:

◆ Reduce costs through reengineered HR administration

◆ Improve service to employees

◆ Increase employees' satisfaction by empowering them with user-friendly technology and information resources

In brief, the HR department needs to transform itself from being a bureaucratic and reactive organization to being a strategic partner that proactively empowers employees to manage their own HR affairs. The transaction-based model of administrative HR has to give way to a new, strategically focused, and empowering model of HR. The strategically-oriented HR department will have more time for program design and competitive initiatives.

The virtual HR professional never forgets that cutting-edge technology provides the mechanism to transform an HR department from being a bureaucratic entity to being a strategic contributor. While a variety of technologies support the self-service model, corporate Intranets excel at enabling the self-service paradigm.

PROFILES OF TWO HR INTRANET PIONEERS

Hewlett-Packard Company

The human resources staff at Hewlett-Packard Company in Palo Alto, California, built an HR Intranet for two reasons. First, the HR staff was required to do more with less. Second, they were mandated to provide even better service than they had in the past. The initial Intranet strategy was aimed at implementing a self-service paradigm at Hewlett-Packard. The goal was to have HR staff answer *fewer* personnel questions and send out *fewer* forms once employees and their managers learned to interact freely with the HR Intranet. This was accomplished. Hewlett-Packard's personnel information home page soon became a vast repository of HR applications, ranging from a button that leads to a drug-testing consent form to a button that provided direct deposit authorization for payroll. The Hewlett-Packard Intranet also included a health plan section that allowed employees to find local participating medical providers who support the employees' medical plans. The Hewlett-Packard Intranet is also expected to evolve into a full-fledged *virtual university* that offers Web-based training curriculums, some of which will be offered by leading universities and training firms. Finally, the Hewlett-Packard Intranet is expected to include expert system capabilities that will recommend training courses to employees to help them eventually maximize their career development potential (Stevens, 1997a).

Eli Lilly and Company

Eli Lilly and Company is a global pharmaceutical company based in Indianapolis, Indiana. It recently launched an HR Intranet that will ultimately provide its workforce with self-service access to HR information 24 hours a day, 365 days a year. The Intranet not only freed up HR professionals from many of their repetitive administrative tasks, but it also played an important role in the company's globalization efforts. For example, in order to coordinate HR initiatives across 116 countries, it became clear that a paper-based distribution system of HR forms, policies, and manuals would not work. Yet by placing HR documentation and manuals on-line and making them accessible over the World Wide Web, Eli Lilly provided the ideal tools that will eventually allow managers and employees to access global and domestic data. That is, Eli Lilly used the Intranet to overcome one of the most complicated technological challenges related to globalizing human resources management: How to allow divergent systems from around the globe to communicate. With an HR Intranet, all that the global sites needed was a Web browser and access to the Internet (Stevens, 1997b).

BUILDING THE HR INTRANET

There is no one blueprint to developing an effective HR Intranet. Yet HR professionals need to learn the basic building blocks for developing an exemplary employee self-service Intranet. The following 10 steps provide such a blueprint.

STEP 1 — *Strategic Intent*

What is the ultimate purpose of the corporation's HR Intranet? Some manageable first steps include establishing a paperless employee self-service system, improving efficiency by using interactive enrollment forms, facilitating corporate communication systems to optimize employee morale, and establishing strategic HR databases that can be mined for competitive advantage.

STEP 2 — *Target Audience*

The virtual HR professional should clearly target the end users of the HR Intranet. Company-wide users could include employees, managers, temporaries, interns, and strategic partners, to name a few. Targeted audience selection helps to shed light on appropriate Intranet promotion strategies along with the the most relevant and appealing HR information content and applications. The trend is to allow Intranet access to all employees.

STEP 3 — *Project Support*

HR managers must develop a vision, plan, and budget for developing the HR Intranet Web site. Senior management must approve the plan and budget. Ideally, an interdepartmental committee of employees and managers will be created to support this important strategic project.

Software Development

The HR Intranet project director will need to select internal and/or external systems analysts and software developers to complete the necessary programming. Excellent off-the-shelf Intranet development software packages can be purchased and quickly installed. Internal or external developers can prepare and configure all content and multimedia components, along with any customized programming requirements.

Content Selection

The HR content must be carefully selected. This includes informational databases and applications. Employees must be impressed with the content they can access on the Intranet if they are expected to visit and support this self-service Website regularly. At a minimum, the site must have all the HR information that employees need to answer their questions. Appropriate content can be selected if HR managers conduct some basic research to determine their employees': (1) most common requests for information, (2) most common problems encountered, and (3) most important expectations concerning the HR Intranet.

Navigational Flow

Once the HR content strategy has been finalized, design experts can begin to detail the navigational flow for the site. For example, *hot buttons* to the most critical HR Web pages should be in full display on the site's home page. Ideally, the Intranet will be built around leading commercial Web browsers that facilitate easy navigation across the many relevant Web pages. Professional designers can be consulted to create elegant and creative screen layouts that require little time to download. Remember that an employee's desire to use the HR Intranet regularly will be based on how attractive it is. Finally, the interface design can include sophisticated yet user-friendly E-mail systems along with interactive forms that are created to be appealing.

STEP 7 | *Usability and Load Testing*

The HR Web site must be thoroughly tested before it goes operational. Any undetected bugs and defects would reflect very poorly on the HR department. *Usability testing* can ensure that employees are able to navigate the HR Intranet easily. *Load testing* is needed to ensure that the Web site can consistently handle the site traffic.

STEP 8 | *Intranet Promotion*

HR managers need to inform employees about the features, functions, and benefits of their company's HR Intranet site. The company's marketing and promotion specialists can provide invaluable advice in this area. To a degree, employees need to be sold on why their work life will become qualitatively better due to the Intranet. Unfortunately, most employees resist change and some employees will not want to make the transition from paper-based to on-line HR systems. Effective promotional strategies could include articles in company newsletters, bulletin board postings, and internal mailings that describe the new Intranet site, and even contests. E-mail broadcasts can also be used to promote the Intranet.

STEP 9 *Integrated Rollout*

Once testing is complete and the HR Intranet Committee has signed off on the system, the HR Intranet can be opened up for business. Early on, high levels of promotion should be maintained to build traffic. Most important, all managers across all divisions and departments should encourage their employees to utilize the Intranet regularly.

STEP 10 *Ongoing Operations*

Finally, a system administrator should make sure that the HR Intranet always runs at peak efficiency and reliability. In addition, the administrator should develop and maintain a disaster recovery plan (e.g., require regular data backups in case of a system crash). Equally important, the virtual HR strategists should regularly check site-generated statistics to assess how often the site is being visited and for what reasons. The virtual HR manager also needs to document that the strategic goals of the HR Intranet are being met (e.g., a significant shift has been documented toward greater employee self-sufficiency). Finally, the HR Intranet Committee must *always* upgrade both the technology and the content that make up the HR Intranet so that visitors are always motivated to visit and use this system.

How Attractive is *Your* HR Intranet?

A CHECKLIST

Yes   No

❏   ❏   1. Does your HR Intranet site convey a clear strategic vision and direction?

❏   ❏   2. Does your Intranet home page draw employees in?

❏   ❏   3. Does the home page design encourage employees to scroll down the page?

❏   ❏   4. Are there appropriate up-front links that allow employees to navigate to the most important Intranet Web pages and sites quickly?

❏   ❏   5. Is the purpose of the HR Intranet site clearly conveyed up front?

❏   ❏   6. Does the HR site's content relate directly to the targeted audience?

❏   ❏   7. Is the Intranet's content relevant and informative?

❏   ❏   8. Is there critical HR information that is missing from the Intranet?

❏   ❏   9. Is the Intranet content poorly written or difficult to understand?

Yes   No

❏   ❏   10. Are the Intranet graphics creative and attractive?

❏   ❏   11. Do all graphics and icons download quickly?

❏   ❏   12. Are all graphics relevant to the HR information being conveyed?

❏   ❏   13. Is the HR Intranet site easy to navigate from one level to another?

❏   ❏   14. Does the Intranet site utilize a logical navigation and search strategy?

❏   ❏   15. Does the Intranet site include an ideal number of levels, or are there too many or too few levels?

❏   ❏   16. Is the HR Web site compatible with the more sophisticated Web browsers?

❏   ❏   17. Is the HR Intranet designed to sustain forecasted traffic?

❏   ❏   18. Is a specific person or committee responsible for the technical support of the site?

❏   ❏   19. Is there an oversight group responsible for the overall security of the site and confidentiality of all on-line HR data and information?

❏   ❏   20. Are all employees Web-enabled to have equal-opportunity access to their HR files and records?

Note: Try to correct any items that received a check in the No column. The very best Intranet Web masters always strive to check the Yes answer across all 20 items.

This questionnaire can also be used as a design guide if you do not already have an HR Intranet.

EMERGING INTRANET TECHNOLOGIES

The next generation of Intranets is already starting to be envisioned, developed, and field-tested. A few of the more promising new technologies for HR Intranets are described below.

1. *Integration with Human Resource Information Systems (HRISs).* A company's core human resources administration system will be made Intranet ready. That is, a company's HRIS applications and databases will integrate smoothly and seamlessly with an Intranet for improved employee self-service and call center integration. Automation without integration would simply reflect a fragmented HR system.

2. *Getting "Pushy."* The emergence of *push* technology, also known as "webcasting," allows company information to be rushed to employees who need it the most. On-line data push technology offers an effective way to broadcast HR data over the Intranet, giving employees instant access to important information without them having to browse through thousands of Intranet pages. Webcasting can automatically deliver production reports, corporate news briefs, and training materials to specified employees. Moreover, this push technology can also deliver personalized news packets from the broader Internet to users' desktops. Targeted webcasting is an excellent strategy for combating information overload. What type of information would you like to receive on a daily basis via webcasting?

3. *Intranet TV.* The near future will probably allow employees to sit in their living rooms while examining their HR Intranet information on their Web TV. This is where Intranet-enabled HR applications are surely headed. Parenthetically, Web-enabled television sets are already being marketed for Internet access.

4. *Extranets.* Corporate Intranets will grow outward, blurring the formal boundaries with the World Wide Web. Extranets will include all corporate employees, their customers, and key vendors, at a minimum. Extranets will have private, firewall-protected sections for HR applications, yet they will also have *common forums* where employees, customers, and vendors might design projects in real time. The maturation of Intranet/Internet development tools, sophisticated messaging systems, and security procedures will fuel the emergence of Extranets. It is even possible that, someday, clusters of compatible companies will share a variety of virtual HR applications and services through an Extranet.

5. *Web-Enabled Videoconferencing.* Intranets of the future will offer Web-based videoconferences. Vendors are already marketing early versions of software that serve up to 100 participants with video, audio, electronic whiteboards, and text-based chat capabilities. The only major obstacle to this form of group interaction on an Intranet is bandwidth limitations.

AVOIDING COSTLY INTRANET BLUNDERS

Virtual HR professionals are skilled at avoiding costly Intranet blunders. The top-10 Intranet blunders are listed below (Callaway, 1997). Rate on a 5-point scale how prepared you feel you are to avoid these blunders (1 = very unprepared; 2 = somewhat unprepared; 3 = in between; 4 = somewhat prepared; 5 = very prepared).

**Your
Preparedness
Rating**   **Blunders**

_____   1. Installing the wrong Intranet applications

_____   2. Underestimating the support requirements for an
                            HR Intranet

_____   3. Solving some but not all of the Intranet security
                            problems

_____   4. Adding HR Intranet applications using poorly designed
                            object architecture

_____   5. Underestimating the network capacity requirements

_____   6. Providing inadequate Intranet management

_____   7. Failing to maintain current and attention-grabbing HR
                            information on the Intranet

_____   8. Relying on weak leadership for Intranet projects

_____   9. Using poorly defined and inadequate database
                            management strategies

_____   10. Going *Web crazy* by putting more content on the Web
                            than can be easily searched and quickly accessed

Total Score = [   ]

Your score should range from 10 to 50. Use the following guide to assess your preparedness to avoid costly Intranet blunders.

Score

10–23   *Low Preparedness.* The odds are high that your company's Intranet will be poorly designed, managed, and maintained.

24–36   *Average Preparedness.* Opportunities for increased preparedness still exist, even though the HR staff is prepared on some fronts.

37–50   *High Preparedness.* This is the range of scores obtained by top-tier virtual HR professionals. These professionals are typically prepared to avoid costly Intranet blunders.

INTRANET RESOURCE WEB SITES

To better understand the evolution of the HR Intranet, many excellent World Wide Web sites exist that can be monitored for Intranet-related white papers. A few of these sites are listed below.

1. Web Week
   URL: http://www.webweek.com

2. Web Master Magazine
   URL: http://www.cio.com

3. Tech Web
   URL: http://www.techweb.com

4. Intranet Journal
   URL: http://www.intranetjournal.com

5. Netscape
   URL: http://www.netscape.com

6. Oracle
   URL: http://www.oracle.com

7. Sun Microsystems
   URL: http://www.sun.com

8. Microsoft
   URL: http://www.microsoft.com

9. Lotus
   URL: http://www.lotus.com

10. PointCast
    URL: http://www.pointcast.com

CHAPTER 4

On-Line Recruitment

ARE YOU READY?

On-line recruiting is still in its infancy. However, the pioneers of virtual HR are already experimenting with this new recruitment paradigm. Answer the following questions to determine if you are a traditionalist or a cyberspace pioneer when it comes to your recruitment style. Please list your current preferences and practices.

	Agree	Undecided	Disagree
1. I prefer to post jobs internally on a standard bulletin board and then list the jobs in the newspaper or relevant trade press.	1	2	3

	Agree	Undecided	Disagree
2. It is easier to use executive recruiters than to post a higher-level job with an on-line career center.	1	2	3
3. I've encouraged my company to develop and/or utilize a home page on the World Wide Web for personnel recruiting.	3	2	1
4. I prefer to physically travel to college campuses to interview student candidates initially, as opposed to receiving their resumes and applications over the Internet.	1	2	3
5. I have utilized a contemporary newspaper that put my job ad on the Internet so that it would become electronically searchable.	3	2	1
6. I prefer to post a job for specialty hires (e.g., software developers, legal professionals, and physicians) on the Web site of a relevant trade publication as opposed to simply printing the job ad in the magazine's help wanted section.	3	2	1
7. I prefer to sort and distribute job applicant resumes quickly by hand than to use resume management software for this task.	1	2	3

8. I have already posted a job with an on-line career center (e.g., Career Mosaic, E-Span, Virtual Job Fair). 3 2 1

9. I have conducted on-line research (e.g., monitoring on-line newsgroups and publications to identify experts) in order to identify job candidates for specialty positions. 3 2 1

10. Quite frankly, I do not understand the strategy or the mechanics of recruiting new employees on-line. 1 2 3

Total Score =

Your score should range from 10 to 30. Use the following guide to gauge your commitment the virtual recruiting.

Score

10–16 *Low Receptivity.* Either on-line recruiting isn't relevant to your current job or you are totally ignoring this new application of HR technology.

17–23 *Moderate Receptivity.* You are at least open to trying some form of electronic recruitment. Your openness will probably increase as this application grows in sophistication and user-friendliness.

24–30 *High Receptivity.* You are committed to the age of electronic recruitment. You obviously want to be at the forefront of this technology-assisted approach to identifying, analyzing, and recruiting highly qualified job candidates.

VIRTUAL STAFFING: A CASE STUDY

Cisco Systems of San Jose, California, always fights with its competitors for the most qualified job candidates (Matlack, 1996). For high-technology companies like Cisco, competitive staffing is a very important strategic goal. Quite simply, the Silicon Valley companies that have the best talent consistently deliver the most competitive products the quickest. Cisco Systems' success with competitive staffing is the result of creative thinking and the use of new recruitment technologies. The key elements of Cisco's virtual HR strategy are summarized below.

1. ***Utilizing Resume Management Systems.*** Resumix is a high-volume resume-processing system that creates a very sophisticated database of qualified job applicants. Using the Resumix system, Cisco quickly scanned and processed anywhere from 1,000 to 2,000 resumes per week. The Resumix system includes patented knowledge-based software to extract critical job-relevant information from the resumes scanned into the system. This job-relevant information forms the building blocks of a comprehensive database of job candidates' skills, experience, education, and job potential. All recruiters and hiring managers at Cisco could then query the Resumix database to identify all of the candidates whose qualifications match the requirements for a targeted job. Finally, a key HR strategy at Cisco was to increase the number and quality of resumes in its database continuously.

2. ***Making Contact on the Internet.*** HR strategists at Cisco Systems realized that their Internet site was an additional place where they could gain an advantage with competitive staffing. First, they created a well-organized Web site that was easy to visit. This meant that job seekers could quickly navigate to the job-posting section with a few mouse clicks. Cisco also used an on-line screening form that required job seekers to

click on a few boxes electronically and then type in a few keywords so that they could immediately view a list of jobs that matched their criteria. Job seekers at Cisco's Web site were therefore able to review many jobs quickly in one visit. Parenthetically, Cisco Systems has even embedded their open job titles into their on-line corporate advertisements to further increase the number of job seekers that are visiting their Web site.

3. ***Launching an Interactive Recruiting Strategy.*** On-line job seekers are also presented with a graphic button that allows them to "make a friend at Cisco." Job seekers complete an on-line form that is sent to a pen pal within Cisco. The job seekers can candidly ask their pen pals about the quality of work life at Cisco. This type of interaction helps job candidates make a more informed decision about applying for a job at Cisco. In addition, the pen pal gets a referral bonus! This strategy allows Cisco to personalize its on-line recruitment efforts in advance of an actual site visit by a job candidate.

4. ***Maximizing Job Fairs with Technology.*** Finally, HR strategists at Cisco realized that technical job fairs would continue to be one of their most productive sources of qualified job candidates. Since the job seekers would also be visiting Cisco's competition at these job fairs, it was important for Cisco to move very quickly to match job candidates to positions and then get them immediately into interview situations. Since Cisco sometimes received as many as 2,000 resumes from one fair, it decided to fax all resumes into the Resumix database directly from the job fair booth. This reduced the amount of time it took to enter these resumes into the system from two weeks to a few minutes. Moreover, the job candidates were quite impressed that their resumes were being entered into the system for immediate matching to open positions. HR professionals at Cisco are truly at the forefront of using on-line technology and data mining to achieve strategic staffing results.

VIRTUAL CAREER CENTERS

A growing number of virtual career centers have opened their doors for business in cyberspace. These on-line job centers update their collection of searchable job postings on a daily basis, and they are engaging in aggressive marketing campaigns to increase their traffic. Many of these centers also educate job applicants on how to prepare a winning resume, properly present themselves in interviews, and link up to a recruiting company's home page to determine if the company's strategic mission fits an applicant's skill set. Virtual HR professionals therefore have an obligation to make sure their company's home page is very appealing to job applicants.

Virtual career centers are obviously an emerging resource for human resource professionals. Companies can list on-line both their domestic and their overseas job openings. Moreover, human resource professionals can electronically search for the ideal candidates since most job applicants tag their resume with keywords that describe their qualifications and interests. Some of the top virtual career centers are listed below, along with their uniform resource locators (URLs).

Adams Job Bank On-Line
URL: http://www.adamsonline.com

Adams Media Corporation publishes books and software to assist job seekers. Their Web site profiles companies that advertise jobs on the site. The Web-site is built around a searchable database that requires job seekers to key in a job title and a preferred location in order to obtain a list of companies with openings. The Web site also includes a resume bank and educational material for job seekers.

America's Job Bank
URL: http://www.ajb.dni.us

This Web site is a joint service of the U.S. Department of Labor and state employment offices. This huge database is based on the available job listings at over 1,800 state employment offices. These job listings contain information such as job descriptions, educational requirements, and necessary work skills. Moreover, this Web site contains links to hundreds of employer Web sites that also contain job listings.

Career Magazine
URL: http://www.careermag.com

This Web site includes tens of thousands of job listings, from major corporations to small businesses. This site contains a resume database, resume searchers, employer profiles, and career-related articles. While this site lists all types of jobs, computer-related and technical/engineering jobs are emphasized. This Web site also provides links to other career-related sites, including salary guides and a directory of employment agencies.

Career Mosaic
URL: http://www.careermosaic.com

This site has truly elegant graphics. It provides a calendar of on-line job fairs. A college connection provides job listings and internships for recent graduates. HR professionals can search a resume database for qualified candidates to fill job openings. This Web site offers an A-to-Z list of companies that lets job candidates familiarize themselves with prestigious corporations. This Web site includes a searchable database of jobs in over 60 different fields, along with several international job databases.

Career Path
URL: http://Lwww.careerpath.com

This site includes hundreds of thousands of job openings in major U.S. cities (e.g., Atlanta, Chicago, Los Angeles, New York City, Washington). This Web site's job database is comprised of listings in the Sunday employment ads from major city newspaper (e.g., the *Chicago Tribune, Los Angeles Times,* and *New York Times*). This site also includes links to each newspaper's home page.

E-Span
URL: http://www.espan.com

This is one of the most complete virtual career centers in cyberspace. It offers employer profiles, job listings, career advice, and motivational articles for job seekers. The heart of E-Span is a large database of job listings that can be searched by occupation, location, salary requirements, education/experience levels, and job description keywords. This comprehensive site also includes links to other job-hunting resources.

Monster Board
URL: http://www.monster.com

The Monster Board is one of the most comprehensive recruitment resources in cyberspace. The main feature of this site is its very large job database. This virtual career center also maintains a very large resume bank. Over 1,500 companies sponsor the Monster Board. It promotes jobs around the world, including in the United States, Europe, and Asia.

On-Line Career Center
URL: http://www.occ.com

This site offers comprehensive employer profiles. Thousands of private and public organizations list their job openings on this Web site. This site offers a range of jobs from entry-level positions for recent college graduates to more advanced positions for experienced professionals. The On-Line Career Center offers resume banks and job listings that are searchable by HR professionals as well as job seekers.

Virtual Job Fair
URL: http://www.careerexpo.com

Over 400 U.S. companies list thousands of jobs on this Web site. Many of these jobs are in the computer and technology fields. This site provides high-quality information and is well organized. It boasts a searchable database of job listings and a resume center that helps job seekers create a password-protected resume. This site provides links to articles and other resources related to technology careers.

ELECTRONIC RECRUITING: SOME CAVEATS

Although the use of the Internet in recruiting is escalating rapidly, human resource professionals need to realize that this form of virtual HR is still in its infancy and experiencing some growing pains. While I feel that electronic recruiting will continue to mature in terms of cost, usability, and quality, there are a few controversial issues that must be taken into consideration. These are briefly listed below.

1. *Developing an Electronic Job-Posting Strategy.* Should you use a virtual career center? These centers usually guarantee maximum across-the-net exposure. Should you use your own Web page? Such a strategy would allow you to collect Equal Employment Opportunity Commission

compliance data easily while showcasing the strengths of your company. Or you might possibly choose to target your job posting to specialty on-line user groups, such as health care personnel (see Med Search; http://www.medsearch.com), legal professionals (see Law Employment Center; http://www.lawjobs.com), and programmers and technicians (see, e.g., Hi-Tech Careers; http://www.hitechcareer.com), to name a few. This latter strategy would ensure that you are connecting with the most relevant type of applicant. The bottom line is that a sound recruiting strategy should be developed before implementing an electronic recruiting plan.

2. *Legal Compliance.* Companies must make sure that they are not adversely discriminating against legally protected subgroups of the population (e.g., racial minorities, applicants 40 years of age or higher). That is, even though companies are broadening their job search through the Internet, there are some concerns that the access to and the use of computers to search for jobs is not consistent across all of society. Currently, those applicants who search for jobs by using Internet sources are predominantly highly educated males, aged 18 to 34, with higher household incomes. Employers who recruit on the Internet run the risk of facing employment discrimination charges if their electronic recruitment strategy attracts Internet users who are predominantly white males. One strategy is to require the collection of EEOC compliance data from on-line job seekers to prove that the pool of job applicants obtained through electronic recruiting matches the area demographics. While companies obviously are not prohibited from using technology for recruitment, the use of the technology must be fair to all subgroups of the population.

3. *Becoming Inundated with Resumes.* It is very easy for applicants to submit their resumes to an on-line job posting. Little more is required than pointing and clicking on the posting. This could lead to an increase in resumes that really do not fit the posted job requirements. Hence, it is very possible that a company will become inundated with resumes

when it posts a job on the Internet. An HR department must then be prepared to acknowledge, store, and track all of these resumes. Needless to say, there will be a booming market for resume management software.

4. ***Quality of Applicant Pool.*** Unfortunately, it is difficult for the virtual career centers to confirm the quality of the resumes and application forms stored in their databases. Human resource professionals could waste a lot of time reviewing and categorizing potentially low-quality resumes. Still, all evidence to date suggests that the top on-line career centers will start to offer more sophisticated on-line tools for reviewing, categorizing, and storing electronic resumes. Moreover, it is anticipated that the on-line recruitment market will eventually center on a handfull of quality-oriented providers that have very large and continuously updated databases. The shake out will help to get rid of the marginal on-line recruiters that provide poor-quality and out-of-date resumes. The future will also include 15 to 20 on-line recruiters who offer specialized services aimed at specific industries.

5. ***Competitive Intelligence Gatherers.*** Human resource professionals need to be aware that their competitors will monitor all of their on-line job postings. For example, if a consulting firm starts to advertise for consultants with health care management experience, then a competitor might accurately deduce that health care management consulting is a lucrative new market. Approval from senior management should be obtained before any strategically sensitive jobs are posted on the Internet.

CHAPTER 5

Computerized Assessments

AN OVERVIEW

Virtual HR professionals are committed to the principles of scientific management. Therefore, they are committed to using only scientifically developed personnel and organizational assessment instruments to quantify a wide variety of job-relevant events, including:

◆ The level and type of knowledge, skills, and abilities that are required from employees to perform successfully in specific jobs

◆ The interest levels that a job applicant pool has for specific job openings

◆ The levels of job knowledge, dependability, and motivation possessed by job candidates and employees

♦ The specific training needs and priorities of key employee groups

♦ Job satisfaction levels across all job levels, departments, and divisions

These HR professionals use computer-based assessment products in order to quickly, conveniently, and economically assess job applicants, current employees, and their organizations. Most of these assessment instruments are not even hand-scorable in any practical sense. That is, they include a large number of diverse assessment items that are scored using scientifically weighted equations. Moreover, the items are summed to yield subscale scores, the subscales are added to form composite scores, and both the subscale and composite scores are taken into consideration when the computer generates a comprehensive profile analysis. These profiles not only indicate if the assessed entity (i.e., an applicant, employee, or organization) is likely to function at a low, medium, or high level of performance, but also identify training and development opportunities.

The very best assessment instruments are based on scientifically developed decision rules. The use of computer-based assessments allows a large number of these decision rules to be executed in microseconds. In addition, research has confirmed that computers are more consistent than humans in following well-defined decision rules. Computers can also be used to administer a wide variety of personnel and organizational assessment instruments. The use of computer-administered assessments not only provides for greater control of the test-taking session, but also makes the scored output immediately available. Moreover, administrator error is greatly reduced. The following section describes the major types of computer-based assessments.

TYPES OF COMPUTER-BASED ASSESSMENTS

Virtual HR professionals engage in a wide variety of computerized assessments. The top 10 types of assessments are summarized next:

1. *Job Analysis Software.* Job experts answer computer-administered and -scored questions that yield a profile of the most important knowledge, skills, abilities, and values required for success in a particular job. Assessment tools that measure these attributes can then be utilized.

2. *Automated Prescreening.* Potential job candidates answer a brief set of questions that assess their interest in and commitment to a specific job offering. Job candidates are typically prescreened through an interactive voice response (IVR) system or through a questionnaire on a company's Web page.

3. *On-Line Interviews.* Job candidates typically answer job-relevant selection questions on a computer at the hiring site. Some automated interviews are conducted over an IVR system, while other forms rely on two-way videoconferencing technology.

4. *Computerized Tests.* Employment test items are computer administered, scored, analyzed, and interpreted. Scientifically-based and valid test profiles are generated. Computerized tests improve both the accuracy and the speed of the assessment process.

5. *Performance Appraisals.* This is a series of computer-based questions that allow managers to rate an employee's job performance qualitatively and quantitatively. Virtual HR professionals can use stand-alone Intranet-based or performance appraisal software.

6. *Training Needs Analysis.* Employees respond to IVR or Intranet-based questions that assess their training needs. Statistical software packages are used to quantify and prioritize the most pressing training deficiencies.

7. *Certification Testing.* More companies are relying on computerized testing centers to administer certification exams that help document

skill mastery and job knowledge attainment. Automated certification testing centers ensure a secure testing environment and are used to computer administer, score, and interpret certification exams. These centers are often used to document mastery of more complex software programs (e.g., Novell's NetWare).

8. *Organizational Surveys.* Employee surveys can be administered over the Intranet or through IVR technology to determine employees' satisfaction and morale levels. The survey data can also be computer scored and analyzed to identify the most dissatisfied employee groups.

9. *Multirater Profiles.* Multirater profiling involves the assessment by an employee's superiors, peers, and subordinates to determine how their perceptions of the employee's job performance differ from the employee's self-perceptions. These assessments are computer administered and scored. A computer-generated profile analysis identifies any gaps or differences in perception between the four categories of respondents.

10. *Exit Interviews.* This can be a response to a series of computer-administered or IVR-based questions. Group reports can be compiled to look for common themes across all acts of employee turnover.

CONDUCTING A COMPUTER-GENERATED JOB ANALYSIS

Virtual HR professionals seek the most accurate information about the knowledge, skills, and abilities that employees need to possess to perform their jobs optimally. This information is essential if HR professionals want to match the right people to the right jobs. In the following case study, a large national convenience store/petroleum marketing chain administered the London House JobVisions system to its key managers. JobVisions is a computer-based job analysis system that translated the managers' input into a computer-generated report that identified which of the following worker traits were most important for job success:

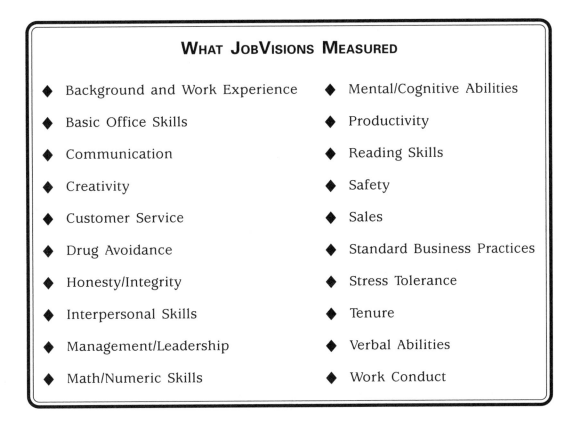

WHAT JOBVISIONS MEASURED

- Background and Work Experience
- Basic Office Skills
- Communication
- Creativity
- Customer Service
- Drug Avoidance
- Honesty/Integrity
- Interpersonal Skills
- Management/Leadership
- Math/Numeric Skills

- Mental/Cognitive Abilities
- Productivity
- Reading Skills
- Safety
- Sales
- Standard Business Practices
- Stress Tolerance
- Tenure
- Verbal Abilities
- Work Conduct

Computer-based job analysis systems like JobVisions are easy to administer. The first step is to select the position a company wants to evaluate. Next, three to five experts answer questions about the targeted job. The questions ask what types of knowledge, skills, and abilities are critically important for success in that job. The survey responses are then computer-scored and analyzed. Most important, the results help companies improve their selection, promotion, and training decisions. The convenience store/petroleum marketing chain gained the following assessment from the JobVisions system.

- JobVisions identified the key skills and attributes necessary for success in a strategically critical position.

◆ This job analysis software enabled the company to create accurate job descriptions.

◆ JobVisions helped the company reorganize positions for improved productivity.

◆ The results helped the company select a preemployment selection test that best matched their employee selection needs.

◆ Most important, it only took a few hours to survey the company's managers and input their data. Once the data were inputted, it took only seconds to receive a computer-generated report that highlighted the most important job requirements.

COMPUTERIZED TESTING APPLICATIONS

Computerized testing is probably the most dominant form of computer-based assessment. Virtual HR professionals use computer-based personnel tests for a wide variety of situations. Some of the major applications are listed below:

1. *Personnel Selection*

   Computer-administered tests are used to evaluate job applicants and to accept or reject them. With personnel selection, a test score leads to a personnel decision that the person hired will be more satisfactory than the person rejected. For example, there are tests that can be used to hire competent managers, successful sales professionals, honest retail clerks, skilled computer programmers, and safe drivers, to name a few.

2. *Placement*

   Automated personnel tests are also used to make accurate placement decisions. While selection tests are used to make a decision to accept or reject each person assessed, in placement decisions no one is rejected. Instead, everyone is assigned to available training programs or jobs to achieve the very best fit between each person's skills and the organization's needs. In placement, a test score predicts that a person will be more satisfactory in one job than in another. Placement is a good strategy when there are fewer candidates applying for a variety of diverse jobs.

3. *Career Counseling*

Computerized career counseling tests can provide employees with useful information about how their thinking styles, work-related personalities, and job-related life experiences can either facilitate or inhibit their career development. With career counseling tests, the test takers can begin to learn how to change their attitudes and behavior in order to better achieve their career goals. They can be taught how to best compensate for their limitations, too.

4. *Training and Development*

Computer-based tests are also used for assessment-based training and development, as well as to identify limitations in an employee's job knowledge and work skills. For example, you can use a test designed to identify management trainees to find out if a candidate has the proper math skills, energy level, and commitment to become a manager. If a person scores poorly in any of these areas, you may recommend a training program to develop the person's business skills, motivation, and attitudes needed for the demanding position. Hence, the test results can be used to prepare an employee for promotion.

5. *Vocational Education*

Automated vocational education tests usually inventory workers' interests. These tests might be used to determine what areas of work students or employees are most interested in, such as mechanical, marketing, managerial, humanitarian, or scientific fields. Vocational education tests can be used to evaluate which occupational titles and activities appeal to a person. Vocational test scores can be combined with other types of tests (e.g., those assessing intelligence and personality) to determine if people's vocational interests match their skills and abilities. If they do match, a person can be encouraged to consider pursuing a particular type of job or career. If they do not match, a person can be motivated to acquire the necessary skills or seek a more compatible job or career.

COMPUTERIZED PREEMPLOYMENT TESTING IN PRACTICE

Preemployment testing is one of the most accurate predictors of employee job performance. When preemployment tests are integrated with computers, the speed and accuracy of the assessment program is further enhanced. Pre-employment tests are typically preferred over other types of screening programs (e.g., resume reviews and traditional interviews) since the tests are more standardized and objective. In addition, Ph.D.-level industrial psychologists oversee the development of computer-based employment tests. Therefore, this type of assessment system is typically based on a solid body of scientific research (Jones, 1994). Industrial psychologists also do everything in their power to ensure that all tests meet current professional and legal guidelines (see Appendix B).

There are a wide variety of computer-based preemployment tests available to business and industry. There are tests that measure entry-level work skills, sales and service orientation, basic supervisory skills, and higher-level managerial and executive potential, to name a few. The three case studies summarized below are based on the London House Personnel Selection Inventory (PSI), a multidimensional computer-based screening test that identifies productive, dependable, and service-oriented job candidates (London House, 1997). The PSI can be computer administered, scored, and interpreted to provide an immediate profile of a job applicant's skills, aptitudes, and motivation. Moreover, through the use of relational databases and sophisticated statistical analysis software packages, a job applicant's scores can be compared with national and/or industry-specific norms. The case studies document the impact of the PSI screening on bottom-line savings for three companies that asked to remain anonymous.

Case Studies

1. FAST-FOOD RESTAURANT CHAIN

A leading fast-food restaurant chain has over 5,000 outlets. It believes that a key to its success is providing high-level customer service while containing costs. Senior executives chose to use the PSI selection test, which predicted customer service orientation along with other job-related characteristics such as tenure, work values, and safety. The company reported an improvement in the overall quality of the employees it hired and a decrease in the average monthly turnover rate from 32.7 to 11.6% after implementing the PSI.

2. DEPARTMENT STORE CHAIN

Department stores experience tremendous loss from inventory shrinkage (i.e., the difference between actual inventory and what the inventory would be if there were no employee theft, shoplifting, damage and waste, and bookkeeping errors). Internal theft accounts for 30 to 70% of inventory shrinkage. A department store chain in the Southwest had an annual shrinkage rate of 2.8% of sales, despite having installed elaborate electronic security devices designed to deter theft. The company's security department decided to implement a PSI integrity test designed to select honest and trustworthy job candidates. During the two years after implementing the computer-based integrity test, the company's annual shrinkage rate dropped to 1.9% of sales—a 33% reduction.

3. RETAIL PETROLEUM MARKETER

A nationally prominent marketer of gasoline and other petroleum products wanted to shift its corporate strategy from a service station orientation to a convenience store strategy. Therefore, it redesigned its service stations to become minimarts with impressive food, beverage, and deli product lines. The company also implemented a PSI preemployment testing program that helped it to hire only highly dependable, drug-free, and service-oriented employees.

The preemployment questionnaire was also designed to capture answers to strategically important recruitment questions such as how the applicants came to apply to the company (e.g., they saw a sign in the window, an employee recruited them, they responded to an ad in the paper). In other words, this company was establishing a small data warehouse that was based on job applicant's test scores, along with their self-report data on how they came to apply for a job at the company.

When this database was mined and statistically analyzed, it was discovered that the more productive and dependable job candidates came from employee referrals, while the more dishonest and counterproductive applicants applied after seeing a sign in the store's window. Needless to say, the latter recruitment strategy was dropped! This case study shows how a computerized employment test can be used to create a strategically useful data warehouse that can be mined for the betterment of the company.

AUTOMATED SCORING OPTIONS

Virtual HR professionals have a wide variety of computerized scoring options for interview, testing, and survey data. Computer-based scoring services are typically fast, economical, and very accurate. Nearly all of these scoring options are available 24-hours a day, seven days a week. Commonly used scoring options include the following:

Telephone Analysis

This scoring option allows immediate evaluation of assessment results with the aid of a telephone and computer. When the personnel assessment is completed and the responses are tallied, the administrator calls the publisher on a toll-free line and reads the responses over the phone. Results are available immediately since an operator accurately keys the responses into computer-based scoring system.

Optical Scanning

A growing number of assessments can be computer scored using optical mark readers. These systems are ideal for companies that want to score multiple assessments on site. For example, in mass-hiring situations, virtual HR professionals might prefer to scan their data into on-site optical mark-reading equipment. The scanned-in data then can be quickly computer scored.

Fax Scoring

Assessments can also be scored using fax technology. For instance, answer sheets that were designed specifically for fax scoring can be faxed to a test publisher using a secure fax machine at both ends. The publisher can then score the responses by computer and fax a completed report to the test user. This system provides complete turnaround results in a matter of minutes.

PC-Based Scoring

With PC-based scoring, personnel assessments can be accomplished quickly using computer-based test administration and scoring software. Concise summary reports can be printed immediately for each assessment scored. These programs offer easy navigation between screens, as well as multiple test administration capabilities and instant on-line help buttons at the test administrator's fingertips.

Interactive Voice Response

With interactive voice response (IVR) technologies, interviews, tests, and surveys are presented telephonically. Respondents are enabled to complete these IVR-based assessments by calling a toll-free number and answering voice-synthesized questions using the Touch-Tone keys on their phones. All test data is then digitally captured and a computerized-scoring program translates this data into useful personnel information (e.g., job applicant profiles and organizational satisfaction levels). Test reports can then be immediately faxed back to the appropriate assessment administrators.

Internet Assessments

While still in its infancy, some Web sites are already capable of administering and scoring organization surveys and interviews on-line. Internet assessment will be a more viable option as the speed of Web browsers increases. Moreover, improved Web-based scoring engines and ways to ensure confidentiality of all data on the Internet are required before this type of assessment platform takes off.

COMPUTER-BASED PERFORMANCE APPRAISALS

Performance appraisals are a key employee assessment and management tool. Nearly all companies conduct such appraisals on their employees. Performance appraisals are routinely used to justify pay adjustments and to determine promotions and terminations. The problem is that 65% of organizations are dissatisfied with their performance appraisal process (Schoenfeld, 1996) because managers find the process too time consuming and burdensome. In addition, employees often feel the process is too subjective and not always job-relevant. The opportunity therefore existed to develop computerized performance appraisal systems that instruct, guide, and assist managers in the appraisal process.

Schoenfeld (1996) reviewed a number of the leading performance appraisal software products. These products were known to reduce the time needed to complete the appraisal process by automating many of the steps and by providing on-line, prewritten texts that can be used to provide quick employee feedback. These systems also increase accuracy and fairness by standardizing all of the critical steps in the process. There are five major product features and functions that should be considered when purchasing a computerized performance appraisal system.

1. ***Installation***—Make sure the end users' computers have enough memory to load the program. Determine if the performance appraisal software can be run on a network. Finally, does the appraisal software support password access only or some other form of security?

2. ***Setup***—Does the performance appraisal software provide a sufficient number of employee file setup fields (e.g., name, job title, grade, location)? Is there also a menu-driven system for choosing the most job-relevant evaluation topics (e.g., job knowledge, dependability, quality management)? Does the software allow for evaluating a broad range of performance? Does the ability to customize exist?

3. ***User Manuals***—Does the software come with well-documented instructions that lead to easy installation and use? Does the manual include examples of how to conduct a computer-assisted performance appraisal along with answers to commonly asked questions? Finally, does the manual include a quick start tutorial that addresses the most important steps in terms of speedy installation and application?

4. ***Help Screen***—Does the performance appraisal software include on-line help features that are very easy to access? Does the program include a search button that allows users to enter the topic they need immediate help with?

5. *User Support*—Finally, does purchasing the product allow access to a technical support staff that can answer questions about performance appraisals in general and the specific software package in particular? Can the support staff be accessed by phone, fax, and/or E-mail? Can new versions of the product be downloaded from the Internet? And is the service staff friendly and courteous?

In summary, performance appraisal software should be easy to install and use. This appraisal software should be a flexible tool that accommodates various formats and performance rating categories. Finally, the appraisal should be professionally sound and legally defensible.

EMERGING ASSESSMENT TECHNOLOGIES

Some niche computerized assessment technologies are starting to surface in the marketplace including these five that have been well received:

1. *Computer-Assisted and Web-Based Interviews.* Software exists that allows a personal computer to act as a first-stage interviewer in the hiring process. Applicants typically make selections from on-screen menus to questions about their job-relevant knowledge, skills, abilities, and work experience. The computer automatically stores answers to each question, follows up on responses to key questions, and computes an overall interview score to aid in personnel decision making. A well-designed computer interview acts as an *expert system* that performs like a trained and experienced interviewer.

Some larger companies are starting to experiment with Web-based video interviews. Hence, corporate interviewers on the East Coast will someday routinely sit "face to face" with a job applicant on the West Coast with the help of two-way videoconferencing programs on the Web. This application will begin to take off once the on-line video presentation rates move from a minimally acceptable 24 frames per second to television quality video that is at least 30 frames per second.

2. ***Computer Telephony-Based Assessments.*** Test publishers are starting to offer brief computer-scored employment tests that are administered over a phone. Test takers are typically required to call a toll-free number and use the keypad on a push-button phone to punch in their answers to the test questions. Answers are scored in seconds by computer and a profile report is faxed back to the test-administering company in minutes. NCS/London House has recently invented a phone-based assessment that measures prospective employees' attitudes toward service, loyalty, safety, drug avoidance, and honesty. This paperless assessment system offers automated test administration and scoring capabilities, immediate results via fax, and multiple report options.

3. ***Computer-Adaptive Testing.*** Computer-adaptive tests tailor an employment questionnaire to individual employees. This is accomplished by having the computer initiate a sequential form of testing in which successive items in the test are chosen based on a respondent's answers to previous items. With this assessment model, the computer continually assesses respondents' competency levels based on their responses to the earlier test items and uses this information to guide subsequent item selection decisions. Computer-adaptive testing, although still being refined for business applications, ends up using fewer test questions while still yielding a very precise test score. This assessment technology should someday have a very big impact in personnel assessment.

4. ***On-line Background and Credit Checks.*** A number of vendors are starting to launch Internet-based services that will allow companies to retrieve job applicants' credit records online. These Web-based reports can provide information such as job-relevant court actions. But before using any on-line credit bureau, make sure it has effective safeguards in place to protect job applicants' privacy rights. The Web sites should also be password protected.

5. ***Computerized Organizational Surveys.*** Software packages exist that allow companies to design fully customized and computerized employee attitude surveys. These software packages rely on a database with hundreds of questions that cover a wide variety of topical areas (e.g., satisfaction with one's boss, job, company). These software programs allow survey data to be collected interactively on disk or over a network. Computer-generated survey reports with a wide variety of breakdown analyses and graphs are produced instantly.

CHAPTER 6

Technology-Assisted Training

VIRTUAL TRAINING AND THE LEARNING ORGANIZATION

Virtual HR professionals realize that creating a learning organization in general and knowledge-proficient workers in particular, are two of the most valuable contributions that virtual training can make to a company's competitive advantage. A corporate knowledge development program must be comprehensive yet very relevant to the company's strategic goals and core competencies. Moreover, developing a knowledge initiative is only half the challenge; reaping competitive advantage through knowledge is the ultimate goal. The four major components required to build a knowledge-based organization are summarized below:

1. **Knowledge Strategy**—Virtual HR managers strive to develop comprehensive strategies for collecting, storing, analyzing, distributing, and using information and knowledge. They try to capture and potentiate high-value knowledge that increases revenue while reducing expenses.

2. *Technology Infrastructure*—Virtual HR managers create streamlined and reliable processes for creating, sharing, using, and updating mission-critical knowledge. Moreover, they use reliable and user-friendly technology to facilitate all knowledge management processes.

3. *Change Management*—Virtual HR managers realize that the transformation of a company from a functional/bureaucratic organization to a competency-based/learning organization is a major change that causes phenomenal stress. Hence, these contemporary managers always implement change management programs that are tailored to meet the needs of a company's specific culture and workforce.

4. *Results Oriented*—Finally, virtual HR managers are results oriented. They will only leverage knowledge via information technology if they know they will obtain a measurable competitive advantage.

Virtual HR managers are very committed to leveraging intellectual capital through information technology. These managers realize that companies must become knowledge-based organizations that can rapidly and continually develop their core competencies if they are to remain highly competitive. Virtual HR managers must therefore ensure that their employees have:

◆ Real-time electronic access to the most up-to-date knowledge databases on topics of competitive importance

◆ Access to decision support and other expert systems that allow faster and better quality decisions

◆ On-line collaboration capabilities through Groupware technology to develop and refine one's business thinking and strategy development

◆ The skills and abilities to use the World Wide Web to find the most relevant educational content across millions of Web sites and Web pages quickly and conveniently

The learning organization is very dependent on virtual training technologies, such as corporate Intranets, interactive multimedia training, and distant-learning paradigms. In fact, the just-in-time delivery of computer-assisted training is an essential requirement of all knowledge-based companies. The following HR objectives of both traditional and virtual HR departments reflect the importance of virtual training to knowledge-based companies.

TRADITIONAL **HR**	VIRTUAL **HR**
1. A comprehensive plan for systematically creating, sharing, and using knowledge does not exist.	1. Virtual HR professionals strategically focus on knowledge acquisition that is integral to competitive advantage.
2. Knowledge usually resides in the minds of a few experts; the company is unable to cross-validate or even disseminate this expert-based knowledge easily.	2. Intranets and Groupware are used to ensure that knowledge is obtained from a collective of the company's best thinkers.
3. Knowledge is kept in employee's desk drawers, file cabinets, or film files.	3. Knowledge is digitally captured, stored, and cataloged for electronic browsing. This knowledge is electronically disseminated to the employees who need it the most at the exact time they need it. Therefore, the just-in-time delivery of training is an essential requirement of all knowledge-based companies.
4. Employees do not regularly access knowledge databases to guide their behavior and improve their decision making.	4. Employees regularly utilize information technology to increase their knowledge. On-line testing and certification helps to confirm that knowledge databases were accessed, studied, and retained.

COMPUTER-ASSISTED TRAINING

Training "multimedia" is typically defined as a set of computer-enabled media such as digital sound, video, and animation, that is integrated with text and graphics to create a very enriched learning experience.

This form of media presentation relies on super-fast computer processors (e.g., Intel's MMX-enabled chips), powerful sound boards, surround-sound speakers, hard drives with abundant storage capabilities, a CD-ROM drive, a high-resolution color monitor, and lots of memory. Multimedia training applications are starting to take off since: (1) multimedia authoring languages are less complicated and less expensive, and (2) desktop computers with multimedia capabilities are now more powerful and less costly.

Multimedia technology and applications are becoming a more frequent choice for corporate training programs. A major reason for this movement is that multimedia training facilitates learning. Remember, employees retain in short-term memory about 20% of what they see, 40% of what they see and hear, and 70% of what they see, hear, and do. Needless to say, interactive multimedia programs challenge the major senses (e.g., seeing and hearing), and they also require trainees to interact with the software.

The technology breakthroughs described earlier in this text (e.g., powerful processors, client–server technology, the Intranet/Internet technologies) have had a major impact on both the scope and flexibility of HR training and development programs. For instance, multimedia training programs can now be delivered on high-powered laptop computers at a fraction of the cost. Distant learning paradigms that rely on Internet transmission of coursework can reduce employees' time off from work and travel costs. Moreover, the distant learning model has a broader global reach. In fact, some of the major benefits of computer-assisted training include:

◆ Improved training accessibility, regardless of time or place. Computer-enabled training can be extended to broader audiences impossible to reach with traditional methods.

◆ Reduced travel costs using on-line or CD-ROM multimedia training, as opposed to expensive classroom training.

◆ More easily customized training delivered at the exact time that the demand for training exists.

◆ Better standardized quality and the consistency of the training message.

◆ Ease of providing more frequent training and ongoing retraining at a reduced cost. Self-paced learning can also be adapted to an employee's strengths and weaknesses.

◆ Reduced learning time (some research suggests by as much as 50%).

◆ On-line assessments that can easily measure actual knowledge mastery, while also providing the metrics needed to track employees' development.

TRADITIONAL VERSUS MULTIMEDIA TRAINING

The following chart contrasts the major elements of an interactive multimedia training program (i.e., text, graphics, audio, video, and animation) with a training program that relies on traditional black-and-white transparencies.

Media Elements	Traditional Training	Interactive Multimedia Training
1. Text	Basic black-and-white type appears on clear transparencies. This presentation is suitable for an overhead projector. Some presenters prefer to use colored text.	Utilizes three-dimensional and multicolored text. Words presented against a multicolored, attention-grabbing background add a creative flare to on-screen phrases. At a minimum, multimedia is projected onto a screen using presentation software (e.g., PowerPoint by Microsoft) and a special projector compatible with the software. However, the text is usually presented on a color video monitor that supports multimedia.
2. Graphics	Simple two-dimensional graphics are used. Some presenters even use hand-drawn figures.	Dynamic, three-dimensional graphics are used. The color of the bar charts or trend lines are varied for impact.
3. Audio	The speaker's voice is all you hear. Digitized audio clips are not used. At best, there will be an animated and exciting presenter. At worst, the presenter will be a bore.	Rich sound comes out of matched stereo speakers. Audio clips are embedded into the multimedia training application file. These clips bring a real-life feel to the seminar (e.g., one can actually listen to

an audio clip of a customer praising an employee). Such audio clips and other sound effects augment the narrator's voice.

4. Pictures

Traditional overhead transparencies are text oriented and rarely include digitized pictures and clip art. These presentations are too left-brain oriented (i.e., the logical and reasoning side) and rarely provide information for the right side of the brain (i.e., the creative and sensing side).

The multimedia program typically includes clip art and digitized pictures. These pictures convey a visual message that is truly worth a thousand words. Multimedia developers can either rely on clip art software that includes thousands of selections and pictures or use flatbed or hand-held scanners to digitize their own collection of art work.

5. Video

There is no video, only a trainer with his or her text-intensive transparencies. A trainer might show a traditional video clip using a VHS player.

Video clips can be strategically placed in the multimedia software program. These clips are activated for a few seconds or minutes during the presentation to create a real-world training experience. The virtual HR professional prefers to use powerful processors that bring multimedia to life, like Intel's MMX technology.

Media Elements	Traditional Training	Interactive Multimedia Training
6. Animation	No animation is possible with traditional training. Boredom is therefore a major risk factor.	Computer-generated animation brings entertaining characters to life on-screen. While some-what costly, animation can reduce boredom and improve attentiveness and enjoyment.

Training Paradigm Exercise

Please recall the media elements used in the last major training program that was conducted at your company. Rate the following six media elements to determine if your company utilizes a traditional training format or an interactive multimedia training format. In addition, compute your average rating. An average score of 3 or less reflects a traditional training orientation, while an average score greater than 3 indicates more of a commitment to a virtual HR training style. Simply circle the numbers that best describe your company's approach to training and then compute your average score.

Training Paradigm

Media Element	Resembled Traditional Seminar		Mixed Model		Resembled Interactive Multimedia
1. Text	1	2	3	4	5
2. Graphics	1	2	3	4	5
3. Pictures/Artwork	1	2	3	4	5
4. Audio	1	2	3	4	5
5. Video	1	2	3	4	5
6. Animation	1	2	3	4	5

Average Score =

Describe a multimedia training program that your company could immediately benefit from:

_____

_____

_____

_____

Virtual Training: Anytime and Anywhere

The following figure is frequently cited by experts in the field of computer-assisted training (e.g., Baisbridge, 1997). It clearly highlights how virtual HR training initiatives can transcend the constraints of time and place. The figure makes reference to *when* and *where* employees can be trained. In addition, more companies are striving to be learning organizations. This means that they are aggressively seeking alternative training paradigms that will extend their traditional training model.

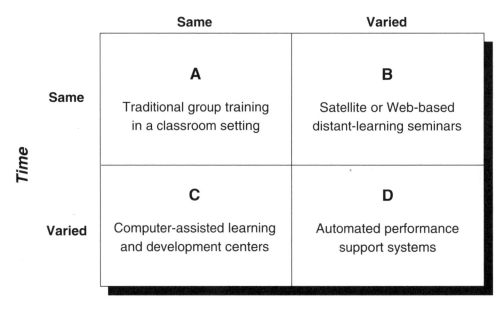

Cell Profiles

A. *Traditional Classroom Training*

This training paradigm involves groups of employees who are trained at the same time and same location. This is the traditional lecture format that is dependent on the knowledge and facilitation skills of the lecturer. At a minimum, virtual HR professionals in this cell use presentation software packages that present vivid text, graphics, sound, and special effects.

B. *Distant-Learning Seminars*

This cell includes a wide variety of cutting-edge distant-learning technologies, including both satellite and Web-based video transmissions. Desktop videoconferencing systems also fall into this cell. As corporations go global, there will be a growing emphasis on distant learning.

C. *Computer-Assisted Learning Centers*

This cell represents training that occurs at the same location yet at different times for different trainees. These automated learning centers are stocked with multimedia computers, standard computer-based training software, interactive multimedia training software, videotapes, and audiotapes.

D. *Performance Support Systems*

This cell represents immediate, just-in-time electronic training. Training applications in this cell have their roots in the help sections built into commercial software. For example, a help screen can be accessed whenever a user of a software application needs immediate help. Hence, training interventions are focused and very brief in this cell. Inexpensive one-to-one desktop videoconferencing systems are also relevant here since they allow an employee to request immediate, just-in-time feedback from a live trainer.

HOW MULTIMEDIA IS USED

A large-scale national survey was recently conducted to determine the prevalence of multimedia-based training in Corporate America (OmniTech, 1996). The OmniTech Consulting Group of Chicago surveyed 146 training managers from Fortune 1,000 companies. Multimedia-based training was defined in the survey as an interactive learning experience incorporating the use of either CD-ROM or World Wide Web technologies. The major findings of this study are summarized below:

1. Multimedia-based training has established quite a foothold in America's largest companies. The average training manager reported that multimedia was used in approximately 16% of employee training hours in 1996. The survey results also suggested that this figure would double by 1998.

2. Approximately 29% of all employees are receiving some form of training via multimedia. The following figure reveals that 30% of all reported multimedia training hours went to professionals. A major reason for the high percentage among professionals is that they have easy access to multimedia computers. All companies should therefore maintain a learning center with multimedia-ready computers that all levels of employees can use.

3. OmniTech also analyzed which departments received the most multimedia training. The results revealed that 81% of the multimedia information services staff, 74% of the sales/marketing staff, 67% of the customer service staff, 67% of the operations/manufacturing staff, and 66% of the human resources staff received multimedia training. On the other hand, only 54% of the product management group, 51% of the finance/accounting staff, 38% of the advertising/PR staff, and 35% of the legal staff received any form of multimedia training. Hence, outside of the information technology group, the groups receiving top priority for multimedia training seem to be those that interface the most with customers.

Multimedia Training by Job Category

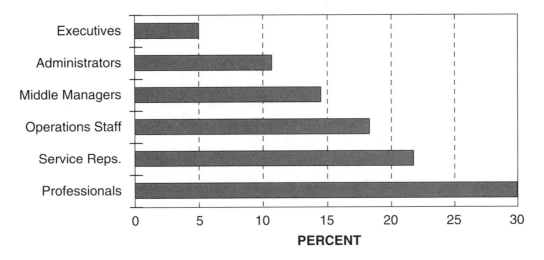

4. One of the most important findings dealt with the courses taught using multimedia. The results revealed that 42% of the respondents used multimedia for training basic computer skills, 25% for technical training, and 11% for advanced computer training. These findings are not surprising since the number one multimedia application has always been to teach the use of hardware and software. Other multimedia subjects included management training (25%), safety compliance (20%), and product training (19%). The next cluster of subjects related to interpersonal skills training (17%), job responsibility training (15%), customer service training (13%), sales/marketing training (13%), and corporate culture training (13%). It is evident that multimedia training is making inroads into a wide range of areas.

5. A full 95% of the responding companies utilize multimedia training on CD-ROM. However, approximately 31% reported that they are distributing some of their multimedia courses on the company Intranets using World Wide Web protocols. The latter percentage is expected to dramatically increase by 1998.

6. The survey also sought to identify the most senior person responsible for multimedia-based training. The results revealed that 73% of the time the person was a manager in a training or human resource function. Yet 15% of the organizations reported that an information technology manager oversaw multimedia-based training. Virtual HR managers must always guard against their authority being usurped by information technology staff. Finally, 70% of the respondents reported that they offer multimedia training through clusters of computers in special learning centers. And approximately 24% reported that their employees had Internet access in 1996 and therefore had the potential to receive Web-based training. It was estimated that, by 1998, 44% would have Internet access.

DISTRIBUTED WEB TRAINING

The future of virtual training will absolutely rely more on Internet-based training (OmniTech, 1996). The Asymetrix Corporation (1997) concluded that the universal adoption of the Internet and, more specifically, the World Wide Web by HR professionals would continue to be driven by four factors:

1. *Universal Access:* The fact that the Web is based on a few simple technology standards—Transmission control protocol/Internet protocol network, Web server software, and Web browser software—will allow the network to continue to grow exponentially. As long as the company has a Web server, it can deliver training content to any employee in the world who has a Web browser.

2. *Ease of Use:* The World Wide Web has made the Internet very easy to use. Moreover, the Web is being refined and enhanced every day. As long as employees have Web browsers and know how to use a computer mouse, they can use the Web effectively, even if they have limited computer experience.

3. *Multimedia Content:* The Web's support for multimedia (e.g., text, graphics, audio, and video) content has enabled the delivery of a wider range of training content. The Web is starting to support even more exotic content (e.g., virtual reality training). These multimedia courses on the Web are available to a diverse and global audience. Moreover, the rich multimedia content is significantly more interesting than traditional content and can therefore hold trainees' attention better. This leads to an improved learning experience.

4. *Intranet Support:* Simply put, an Intranet is the use of Internet and Web technology as the basis of an organization's internal network. An HR department has complete control over its Intranet-based applications. This includes network performance, security, and even cost management. The future will surely yield an almost seamless integration between a company's Intranet and the Internet. This means that employees can be receiving immediate, company-specific training on their Intranet, yet can also be immediately hyperlinked into the Internet if they require supplemental training.

The World Wide Web is the most exciting new medium for delivering interactive multimedia training. This new form of virtual training is referred to as "distributed training" (Asymetrix Corporation, 1997). Distributed training is defined as the use of computer and Internet technologies to manage the delivery of training programs to a dispersed group of employees.

Distributed training provides the same benefits afforded by traditional computer-based training: lower costs, decreased learning time, and higher retention rates. Yet the use of the Internet to deliver distributed training provides additional benefits, including lower development costs, lower distribution costs, and ease of certification (Asymetrix Corporation, 1997):

1. *Lower Development Costs*: The World Wide Web relies on a common set of industry standards (e.g., HTML, Java) for developing applications. What makes the use of these standards so powerful is the fact that

applications based on them run independently of the computer platform and operating system on which they run. By developing a course based on HTML and Sun Microsystems' Java, for example, a course developer need only create one training module. That same module will run on any computer platform, including Windows, Macintosh, and UNIX. All that is necessary is that the course be accessed with the proper Web browser (e.g., Netscape Navigator or Microsoft Internet Explorer). Parenthetically, traditional computer-based training typically relies on CD-ROM technology that requires a different version of the course for every computer platform used. This constraint is very costly.

2. ***Lower Distribution Costs***: Once a training module has been installed on a Web server, it becomes immediately accessible by any employee in the world who has both Internet access and a Web browser. When a training course needs to be altered, a virtual HR professional can quickly make the changes and update the Web server with the new version. Conversely, with traditional, computer-based training, it is often necessary to manufacture and deliver CD-ROMs for every user being trained. In addition, there are major costs associated with installing and maintaining the computer-based training course on all employees' personal computers. The costs associated with this type of distribution prohibit the frequent updating and improvement of training modules.

3. ***Easy Certification***: The Asymetrix Corporation (1997) points out that the Internet is the only medium, other than the telephone, that supports two-way communication. With distributed training, virtual HR professionals are able to take advantage of this two-way communication to track the performance of every trainee. Moreover, by capturing on-line training performance data, virtual HR professionals can measure the overall effectiveness of a training program and improve it based on the results. Finally, employees' can be administered an on-line certification test to document the attainment of job knowledge. This form of electronic certification testing immediately documents training effectiveness.

Return on Investment

From a cost-savings analysis, the Asymetrix Corporation (1997) found that in a typical training scenario, computer-based training delivers a 3% savings over traditional classroom training during the first year of implementation. In year two, computer-based training delivers a 26% savings over classroom training. By taking advantage of the Internet to deliver training, the Asymetrix Corporation found that Internet-based training delivers a 23% savings over traditional classroom training during the first year, and a 43% savings in year two. These figures clearly support the promise of these two virtual training applications.

WEB-BASED TRAINING: A CASE STUDY

Web-based training involves the use of educational applications that integrate hyperlinked text and graphics, brief on-line video clips, and interactive mastery testing. Web-based training brings the classroom to the end user's desktop, thus eliminating costly travel. Web-based training is not static like the traditional forms of training (e.g., computer-based training).

With Web-based training, users can access their courses to answer a single question or to study an entire curriculum. Moreover, employees can access this on-line training system 24 hours day, 365 days a year. Multiple-choice knowledge acquisition tests can also be administrated over the Web to document that the employees did indeed learn their coursework. Web-based training content can be continually improved, enriched, and expanded. In fact, the training content on the Web server can be easily updated so that all employees can immediately access the updated content. A trainer no longer has to worry about recalling floppy disks or CD-ROM's.

Callaway (1996) describes a Web-based training application at General Motors Corporation. General Motors training strategists did not feel that their employees had to fly halfway across the country to learn job skills and strategies. Instead, they felt that job-relevant education could be brought to these employees' desktops over General Motor's corporate Intranet. Therefore, General Motors training strategists designed a Web-based training program that would be accessed by approximately 600 General Motor Service Parts Operations managers in about 500 locations across the United States. These managers will be able to access training modules that address topics such as how to run a profitable General Motor dealership and how to provide outstanding customer service.

DESIGNING VIRTUAL HR TRAINING PROGRAMS

Managers take great care in developing virtual HR training programs. Whether they are designing training programs for interactive CD-ROMs or Web-based delivery, they rely on 10 guiding principles of exemplary training program design. How many of these principles do you adhere to?

Yes No

☐ ☐ 1. Do you rely on a formal development process that meets the most critical training needs of your employees?

☐ ☐ 2. Do you choose the media types and formats (e.g., text, graphics, audio, video) based on how well they will help you meet your training objectives, as opposed to their glitzy effect?

☐ ☐ 3. Do you always strive to make your virtual HR training experience as interactive as possible to engage your employees fully?

☐ ☐ 4. Do you supplement your basic training content with other available information resources (e.g., hyperlinks to related Web pages, access to on-line multiple choice questions that challenge learners)?

❏ ❏ 5. Do you design your training systems to accommodate the fact that employees learn in a wide variety of ways? That is, do you use a wide variety of diverse strategies and exercises within your technology-assisted training application?

❏ ❏ 6. In the age of information overload, do you avoid at all costs training content that is too lengthy, irrelevant, or unfairly difficult?

❏ ❏ 7. Do you avoid using the outdated "beginning to end," "left to right," or "top-down" models of training, and instead design your training so that learners can directly go to the sections that they want to master? For example, can employees "drill down" to learn about a topic in more depth, and can they take advantage of hyperlinks to jump forwards and backwards to related topics of interest?

❏ ❏ 8. Do you always test out and revise your training content with beta groups of employees before loading it into your software systems?

❏ ❏ 9. Do you always make sure your training technology is user-friendly?

❏ ❏ 10. Finally, do you always evaluate the effectiveness of your virtual HR training application on corporate financial performance and employee productivity?

VIRTUAL REALITY TRAINING

Virtual reality is a computer-generated artificial reality that projects employees into a three-dimensional space generated by a head-mounted or desktop stereoscopic display. The experience oftentimes utilizes data gloves that allow employees to manipulate illusory objects in their environment. Hence, virtual reality training provides a highly interactive environment in which exploration by trainees is encouraged. Virtual reality training simulates reality by providing a nonlinear, user-directed training experience in which employees can take actions and see the consequences of their actions, just as they would occur in the real world.

Virtual reality relies on computers and other special hardware and software to generate the simulation of an alternative world. Since employees are able to actually practice their job in a simulated world, this can save a lot of time and money when it comes to doing the job in the real world. Virtual reality seems so realistic to trainees because the system allows our brains to sense the simulated world by presenting it to our senses through virtual reality output and input devices. Output devices change electronic signals into physical phenomena. An example of this would be the head-mounted display through which the virtual reality user sees. The virtual reality input devices also measure and record the physical happenings electronically, and so create digital signals that the computer can read. Examples of input devices include a keyboard and a mouse (or data gloves) that participants use to maneuver through their simulated world.

Nina Adams (1996) is a pioneer in developing and implementing virtual reality training programs. Her consulting group developed multiple virtual reality training applications for use by Motorola to train employees on how to operate high-tech manufacturing equipment. Adams initially used Superscope Virtual Reality software to develop her programs. Adams indicates that virtual reality training provides a very safe learning environment for employees since the computer-simulated experience does not bring harmful risk to people or equipment. (Parenthetically, that is why the earliest virtual reality applications were conducted in the aerospace and the medical/surgical fields.)

Adams's research has shown that virtual reality training increases user confidence, reduces time to proficiency, and increases worker consistency. More specifically, at Motorola she developed, implemented, and studied a virtual reality environment that replicated a multiphased, high-tech assembly line. She developed a desktop virtual reality environment that could be freely navigated, interacted with, and viewed from a near infinite number of perspectives. She found that assembly line workers who were immersed and trained in this computer-simulated virtual reality environment made 93% fewer mistakes than employees who received the standard, real-world training, which consisted of seminars and hands on experience. Some other highlights of this study include the following:

1. Traditional training required access to the actual manufacturing line, so that trainees at remote sites were unable to receive full training. However, with virtual reality everyone received full training since they easily gained access to the virtual manufacturing line developed by Nina Adams.

2. The development and implementation costs for the virtual reality training did not cost any more than traditional multimedia training programs, despite the fact that the virtual reality program came closer to simulating reality. In fact, the virtual reality program allowed for maximum interaction when compared with other training programs (e.g., lectures allow for minimum interaction, while computer-based training encourages moderate interaction). Higher levels of interaction should lead to quicker learning and higher retention rates.

3. When the virtual reality program was used as a stand-alone training module, trainers' salaries, travel expenses, and facility costs were lower compared with those of the traditional training model.

In summary, there surely will be an increase in virtual reality training programs. In fact, Adams cited studies suggesting that approximately 20% of the companies surveyed by the American Society of Training and Development specifically mentioned that virtual reality would be a high-priority training technology for them in the near future. In fact the virtual reality program was so well received at Motorola that the company decided to have the Adams Consulting Group develop additional virtual reality training programs, including one for robotics. If NASA used virtual reality to help train astronauts to handle emergencies in space, then the application of virtual reality training in business and industry is unlimited.

TRAINING MANAGEMENT SOFTWARE: A CASE STUDY

Virtual HR training activities must be judiciously monitored and managed. For example, Duracell's corporate education and development group implemented a training management system to keep track of the development of over 9,000 employees throughout the world (Warek, 1997). The task force assigned to develop this training system consisted of Duracell's manager of training systems and services, the corporate HR information system manager, the multimedia information systems manager, and other members of Duracell's Training and Advisory Board.

Duracell needed such a system since it had no systematic way to record and track company-wide training activities. There was also no computerized system for scheduling and enrolling trainees. Finally, there was no system for documenting individual development plans and training certification. In brief, Duracell was unable to manage effectively the planning and delivery of company-wide training services. Duracell's training task force wanted one common system that would address the following system objectives and desired functions.(Warek, 1997):

SYSTEM OBJECTIVES

◆ Provide an accurate reporting of world-wide training activities and cost.

◆ Provide a consistent framework for reporting all training activities.

◆ Interface with other HR applications used for succession planning and performance management.

◆ Coordinate and manage training services to ensure the delivery of a high quality program.

◆ Provide a user-friendly system.

DESIRED FUNCTIONS

◆ Schedule courses and manage logistics.

◆ Track enrollment for internal courses.

◆ Retrieve information/reports.

◆ Generate correspondence/certificates/tent cards/name tags.

◆ Monitor budget and expenditures.

◆ Link curriculum to positions, competencies, and courses.

◆ Prepare training and development plans.

◆ Track external and tuition reimbursement activities.

The Duracell task force evaluated 12 different training management and tracking systems against the desired functions and objectives and selected the Training Administrator software package by Gyrus Systems, Inc. Duracell's task force met with a Gyrus representative to devise a rollout strategy consisting of system development, testing, and security, along with administrator training. The system was gradually rolled out and a project manager was assigned. The training management system immediately helped with training enrollment, scheduling, course coordination, and evaluation. This training-related information management system will be a critical element in Duracell's strategy to become a competency-based organization.

CHAPTER 7

Becoming a
Virtual HR Professional

This chapter addresses eight critically important areas that HR managers and professionals must master before they can become full-fledged virtual HR superstars.

1. DEVELOPING 21ST-CENTURY JOB SKILLS

Virtual HR professionals must develop a contemporary workplace style if they plan to succeed in the reengineered and automated world of human resources management. They must have a solid "Can Do/Will Do" approach to their jobs. That is, they must be intelligent enough about strategic human resources management and information technology applications to reinvent and then operate a virtual HR program at their company. This is the "Can Do" part of the job. In addition, they must be able to work with teams, cope with a rapidly changing workforce, and maintain a high level of productivity at all times. This is the "Will Do" part of the job. The five most important personality traits of a successful virtual HR professional are listed below. Use the rating scale to indicate how much of these traits you possess (1 = very low; 2 = low; 3 = average; 4 = high; 5 = very high).

———— 1. ***Gold-Collar Work Ethic***—This is the ability to have multiple specialties and not be too narrowly focused in one's job skills. Gold-collar workers are willing to take on the most challenging projects, especially projects like reengineering the HR department in the Information Age. Gold-collar workers also embrace an innovative and solution-oriented thinking style. They always accomplish what they set out to do, and they can work on multiple projects simultaneously.

———— 2. ***Managing Chaos***—This is the ability to work in highly demanding and challenging work environments. Virtual HR professionals patiently and intelligently bring order out of chaos. Most important, they are able to work in a highly demanding work environment without burning out or experiencing information overload, and so must master a wide variety of stress coping skills.

———— 3. ***Team Orientation***—Most of the major phases involved in reengineering the HR department involve teamwork. Therefore, virtual HR professionals must be highly skilled at working within and oftentimes leading project management teams. Such professionals must also be able to resolve team conflicts diplomatically.

———— 4. ***Empowerment***—Virtual HR professionals must engage high levels of teaching, coaching, motivating, and, most important, trusting, all of which exemplify empowering others. After all, the self-service paradigm is at the heart and soul of the virtual HR movement.

_____ 5. *Self-Direction*—Virtual HR professionals must be skilled self-managers. This is critical since the professional's workload will be high yet the available resources will be scarcer. Finally, there must be lifelong commitment to continuous learning and self-education.

Average Score = [   ]

2. COPING WITH GROWING TECHNOLOGY DEMANDS

HR professionals need to become significantly more sophisticated in terms of their technology and information management skills. A humbling experience for any HR representative is to read a listing of job ads in the human resources section of a major newspaper. These ads look like they belong in the computer programmers and systems analysts section of the paper! For example, I recently read two ads in the HR section of the *Chicago Tribune*. One ad asked for a human resources representative while the other ad asked for an associate in HR systems support. Both ads were seeking HR specialists who had the following technical skills:

◆ PC proficiency

◆ HR information system expertise

◆ Database management skills

◆ Automated report generation skills

◆ Statistical analysis abilities

◆ Communication and presentation skills

HR professionals must also learn how to manage the reengineering process that culminates in a virtual HR department. That is, they must know how to identify, chart, and then automate the mission-critical HR functions. They must also be skilled at developing information security policies to protect the integrity and confidentiality of on-line personnel databases. Virtual HR professionals must also help ensure that their employees' skill sets are keeping pace with the growing technology demands. If the workforce is not technologically savvy and literate, it will struggle with the self-service model introduced through virtual HR. Finally, virtual HR professionals must be very skilled at managing change and resistance associated with the radical reengineering of major HR processes, functions, and paradigms.

Such professionals must also increase their knowledge of, and ability to implement, a strategic HR plan. If fact, as HR professionals move away from their administrative role, they will move toward a more strategic role in the company. For example, HR professionals must be skilled at knowing how to transform their company from a functionally-oriented organization to a competency-based enterprise. They need to know how to redesign overly bureaucratic organizations into flatter, horizontally networked companies. They must also be wizards at successfully rightsizing or smartsizing their organization and know how to hire, train, and retain knowledge-competent workers who will help a learning organization reach its full potential. Virtual HR professionals must implement only those processes and procedures that help their companies work smarter, faster, and more productively.

Finally, such professionals must always be fully prepared to succeed in a cyber-workplace. They should never deny the importance that technology will play in redefining the human resources processes and functions, and thus must accept the following premises as truth so that they are never caught off guard in the future:

◆ Global computer networks will continue to proliferate.

◆ Those who are cyber-savvy will gain advantage at work.

◆ Advances in information technology will threaten many HR jobs.

◆ All HR skills will become obsolete faster.

◆ Becoming a virtual HR professional increases one's survival rate in the future.

3. BECOMING A MASTER OF CHANGE

To become a competent virtual HR professional, one must be an outstanding negotiator, strategist, and overall master of change. These skills are needed in order to transform the corporate culture, reengineer HR departments, and procure the use of financial, technological, and human resources. An HR professional must be able to overcome any obstacle in his or her way. The following scenario reflects the actions that an HR professional must take to launch a virtual HR initiative at his or her company successfully:

1. Gain executive support for a virtual HR unit.

2. Become involved in corporate strategy planning.

3. Provide solid HR leadership.

4. Receive access to cutting-edge information technologies and resources.

5. Bring documented value and competitive advantage to the company.

HR representatives will fail in this pursuit if they:

1. Have poor strategy formulation and planning skills.

2. Lack close relationships with senior executives.

3. Continually fail to meet their key goals and commitments.

4. Do not really understand the company's business environment.

5. Are not perceived to be a critical resource within the company.

What personal skills and abilities do you possess that will help you to gain the support and resources necessary to build a virtual HR enterprise?

_____

_____

What personal limitations or skill deficiencies do you need to overcome before you can obtain the support and resources to develop a virtual HR department?

_____

_____

4. LEARNING PROJECT MANAGEMENT SKILLS

Virtual HR professionals need to master project management skills. For example, they must help their organizations decide if they should develop a virtual HR system in-house or if they should outsource all or part of the project. Such professionals never bring a development project or service need in-house if they lack the expertise to provide that service in a timely and cost-effective manner. They must also be able to offer guidance to the legal department on how to put together a comprehensive contract that protects their company's business interests. The following questions assess whether you and your company have the skills to develop virtual HR projects. (Circle the appropriate answer.)

Requirement	Yes (In-House)	Uncertain (Find Out)	No (Outsourced)
1. Does your company have the staffing resources to assign to the project?	Yes	?	No
2. Are such staff able to design and develop the virtual HR application or service?	Yes	?	No
3. Does your company have the expertise to conduct an accurate needs analysis to identify the most promising virtual HR programs?	Yes	?	No
4. Is your company capable of designing, implementing, and analyzing a field test of the virtual HR application?	Yes	?	No
5. Can your information technology group provide the hardware, software, and/or computer/telephone systems required by the virtual HR application?	Yes	?	No

Requirement	Yes (In-House)	Uncertain (Find Out)	No (Outsourced)
6. Are company training staff available to teach employees and managers how to use the application?	Yes	?	No
7. Are there internal marketing resources and corporate communication strategies that can be used to promote and roll out the program effectively?	Yes	?	No
8. Is staff available to maintain, update, and possibly modify the virtual HR applications?	Yes	?	No
9. Is your company committed to using a team-oriented approach to designing, developing, and implementing the program?	Yes	?	No
10. Are you skilled at using project management software to track your progress and stay on schedule and within budget?	Yes	?	No

Five of the most important reasons virtual HR projects fail are: (1) Inferior or poorly defined ideas are accepted as viable projects; (2) the development team sets unrealistic project deadlines; (3) an underskilled project manager oversees the project; (4) the project is not broken down into workable chunks; and (5) a clearly delineated plan is not developed. The following worksheet can be used to improve virtual HR planning.

PROJECT MANAGEMENT WORKSHEET			
Virtual HR Project Steps	**Person(s) Responsible**	**Due Date**	**Success Factors**
1. Team configured			
2. Project scope defined			
3. Project scope approved			
4. Existing HR process delineated			
5. Virtual HR process defined			
6. Virtual HR process approved			
7. Resources obtained			
8. Development begins			
9. Development completed			
10. Implementation plan approved			
11. Implementation completed			
12. Performance audit occurs			

5. EXCELING AT STRATEGIC HR RESEARCH

Virtual HR professionals must become research experts. This is especially important since there will be increasing demands on HR staff to provide high-level strategic input. Three levels of research skills are recommended: (1) They can subscribe to on-line individualized news services so they can stay abreast of late-breaking stories with HR implications; (2) they should acquire some degree of expertise in terms of HR data warehousing, mining, and statistical analyses; and (3) they should be able to conduct targeted research on the World Wide Web. In brief, such professionals cannot shy away from their research responsibilities of turning data into information. Each of these three research fronts is briefly summarized below.

Individualized HR News Briefs

Virtual HR professionals are encouraged to get their own individualized, computer-generated news briefs each day and thus capture late-breaking news from the world's most authoritative publishers and information organizations.

Personal news briefs rely on intelligent technology filtering and a comprehensive database of highly credible news stories to allow HR professionals to receive timely, focused, and personally relevant news. This saves time and prevents information overload. Companies such as Yahoo! (URL: http://www.yahoo.com), Individual, Inc. (URL: http://www.newspage.com), and PointCast (URL: http://www.pointcast.com) provide this service. Other benefits include the abilities to:

◆ Access HR news stories that one wouldn't ordinarily see

◆ Save time and start each day with strategically relevant information

◆ Become the HR information expert in your office

♦ Spot emerging HR trends and potential crises

♦ Monitor technologies that will have immediate or future applications to virtual HR

Data Warehousing and Mining

These days, virtual HR professionals must become very skilled at turning HR data into better business decisions. These professionals realize that within their massive HR databases are secrets that can be mined to make their company more competitive and profitable. Data mining is the analytical process that brings those secrets to the surface. HR departments are ripe for data warehousing and mining applications since nearly all HR transactions and business events are recorded in databases. This information can be statistically analyzed and modeled for better HR decision making (SAS Institute, 1995).

A data warehouse is a large repository of HR data that comes from all levels of employees involved with all types of transactions. The data is collected over time and forms the basis for computing comparative analyses, trends, and forecasts. The five steps for building an HR data warehouse are:

1. Conceptualizing the breadth and scope of a strategically relevant database.

2. Developing strategies and programs for coding, storing, and extracting data from the data warehouse.

3. Developing statistical rules for dealing with problem data and for standardizing data sets.

4. Setting up methodologies for reviewing the quality of the data in the warehouse and for cleaning up the database if needed.

5. Ideally, setting up programs for electronically loading data into the warehouse.

Data Mining Flow Chart

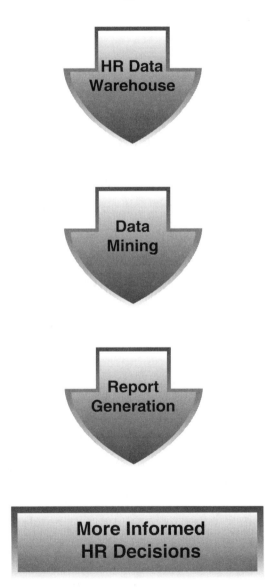

The next step is to mine and analyze the data for competitive advantage. Data mining is defined as "advanced methods for exploring and modeling relationships in large amounts of data" (SAS Institute, 1997, p. 2). Powerful statistical analysis packages can be used to query, analyze, model, and report on this database. The goal is to extract key facts and statistical relationships from the available data to facilitate better business decision making.

Data can be extracted from a data warehouse and analyzed using statistics such as multiple regression analysis, discriminant analysis, cluster analysis, and time series forecasting, to name a few. These analyses would allow virtual HR professionals to better understand relationships between variables.

Conducting Research on the Web

Virtual HR professionals can "surf" the World Wide Web to find current, accurate, and immediate answers to most of their corporate strategy questions in general and HR questions in particular. The World Wide Web is full of meaningful information that is growing exponentially in volume each day. Cahlin (1997) reported that there are nearly 70 million Web pages, tens of thousands of news groups, and millions of people sharing information on the Web. Yet virtual HR professionals must master search engines if they want to organize meaningfully all of the data on the Web so that it becomes useful information.

Internet-based search engines hunt down and retrieve on-line information. Based on a query or keyword search request, a search engine delivers a list of Web sites that match the query. Popular search engines include:

◆ Yahoo! (URL: http://www.yahoo.com)

◆ Excite (URL: http://www.excite.com)

◆ Lycos (URL: http://www.lycos.com)

◆ Infoseek (URL: http://www.infoseek.com)

◆ Hot Bot (URL: http://www.hotbot.com)

These search engines and others are able to identify, categorize, and rank the information that matches the keyword search. HR professionals can then scroll through the list to determine which web sites are most relevant to answering their questions.

For example, lets say the research question relates to how companies can optimally comply with the Americans with Disabilities Act (ADA). The virtual HR professional could use the Yahoo! search engine and enter a keyword or phrase that best describes the search objectives. In this case the phrase entered could simply be "Americans with Disabilities Act." Yahoo! first allows a person to search specific databases and then provides a list of hyperlinked Web sites relevant to the ADA. The list would include the title of the site, the universal resource locator, and a brief summary of the information that is available. Virtual HR professionals could then visit these sites and print out all relevant research reports. The use of Web browsers and search engines definitely provides an invaluable research tool for HR professionals. Other useful Web sites for HR professionals are summarized below.

Web Sites for HR Professionals

American Society for Training and Development (ASTD)
URL: http://www.astd.org
This site describes ASTD's mission, products, and services. It also provides a table of contents and abstracts of the most recent issues of Training & Development magazine and the results of an annual survey that ASTD conducts on the training industry. This information should be valuable to trainers and

market researchers alike. Finally, this site offers information on ASTD conferences, memberships, and related services.

Human Resource Executive
URL: http://www.workindex.com

This Web site is offered by *Human Resource Executive* magazine in conjunction with Cornell University. This site provides an excellent gateway to many of the best work-oriented Web sites on the Internet. The sites are indexed by over 25 major subject categories, including: (1) technology and software; (2) testing, appraisal, and evaluation, and (3) training and development. This site provides scientific studies, legal decisions, association news, and even supplier information, all pertaining to the workplace.

International Association for Human Resource Information Management (IHRIM)
URL: http://www.ihrim.org

This site is fast becoming *the* Web site for virtual HR specialists. The IHRIM site provides the information that HR professionals need to tackle the complex issues surrounding today's technology. This site provides access to special interest groups dedicated to specific areas of HR interest. One of the most exciting groups is the Global Special Interest Group, which facilitates the sharing of information about global business, regulatory data, and technology matters relating to human resources. The HR System Center provides software surveys, buyer's guides, and product search tools. Access to key HR information system articles from this association's trade magazine is also available. For example, an on-line article from the February–March 1997 issue is entitled, "Strategic Outsourcing: Options, Issues and Strategies for HRIM." IHRIM members can also order the latest books on technology-assisted human resource management from this site.

Society for Human Resource Management (SHRM)
URL: http://www.shrm.org

This is the first place to go to find anything related to human resources on the Web. This comprehensive site includes: (1) listings of conferences, seminars, and other educational events being offered across the country; (2) products, services, and even a buying guide, organized by functional HR area (e.g., compensation/benefits); and (3) membership services and information. This site also provides links to other HR sites on the Web, by category.

Society for Industrial-Organization Psychology (SIOP)
URL: http://cmit.unomaha.edu/TIP/TIP.Ltml

This is the Web site of the *The Industrial-Organizational Psychologist,* or *TIP,* the newsletter of the Society for Industrial-Organizational Psychology. This newsletter contains commentaries on a wide variety of contemporary HR topics. A recent on-line *TIP* issue included articles such as "Industrial/Organizational Psychology in the Web Age" and "Traveling in Cyberspace: Computer-Based Training." Virtual HR professionals can also download timely research reports (e.g., "Affirmative Action: A Review of Psychological and Behavioral Research").

Yahoo! The Business and Economics Section
URL: http://www.yahoo.com

Yahoo! is one of the most popular global search engines on the Internet. Virtual HR professionals can click on the business and economics section and gain access to thousands of prequalified, high-caliber topics on personnel management, computer technologies, and strategic management. At this site, professionals can design their own personalized electronic newspaper, covering only highly relevant topics and therefore better manage their time.

U.S. Equal Employment Opportunity Commission (EEOC)
URL: http://www.eeoc.gov

The EEOC is one of the most important regulatory agencies that virtual HR professionals must stay informed about. For example, these professionals must always strive to choose valid, reliable, and fair assessment instruments so that they can fully comply with the employment laws enforced by the EEOC. This Web site provides fact sheets related to EEOC regulations along with amended copies of all the laws enforced by the EEOC (e.g., the Civil Rights Act of 1991, sections of the Americans with Disabilities Act of 1990). The site also includes all of EEOC's recent press releases.

6. PRACTICING RISK MANAGEMENT

Employees who use virtual HR technologies to access corporate information have an ethical and legal obligation to protect this business information. In fact, they must constantly practice risk management by educating their employees about the company's information security policies. Moreover, all employees should sign an agreement form indicating that they have read all policies concerning access to and protection of the company's computer systems and the information they contain. Some common security procedures that should be covered in these policies include the following:

Logging In—Access to the computer systems should be authenticated with a password. In addition, all passwords should have a limited lifespan and be changed regularly.

Logging Off—Employees should always log off before they leave their computer unattended.

Remote Access—Only select employees should be granted permission to access their company's computer systems remotely. These employees should assume full responsibility for ensuring that they do not introduce a harmful virus into the system. They should also prevent any intruder from accessing the corporate systems through their remote system.

On-Line Service—Employees should consult with the information technology department before establishing any account with on-line service providers. If permission is granted, the on-line service should be used only for corporate purposes unless permission is granted otherwise.

External Files—All downloaded files from external computer systems should be decontaminated for viruses using high-quality virus protection software. Prior approval should be granted before downloading any file from any external computer.

Emergency Access—An authorized business manager should approve all emergency access to a computer system, network, on-line service, or corporate database. All cases of emergency access to another employee's computer should be closely monitored.

Security Breakdowns—It is an employee's responsibility to immediately report all security breakdowns to the information technology department.

Information Security Policy—Employees must thoroughly study and adhere to the company's information security policy. A standard policy prevents:

◆ Destruction of corporate hardware, software, and data

◆ Illegal copying of third-party software

◆ Theft or loss of proprietary corporate information

◆ Unauthorized access of confidential personnel data

◆ Mismanagement of sensitive corporate information. In fact, access to such information should be restricted if necessary.

Minimizing Legal Exposures

As part of their risk management responsibilities, virtual HR professionals must first try to minimize all legal exposure and then insure themselves against any such exposure (Wilder, 1997). A high score on the following questionnaire reflects a strong security orientation that should safely reduce the risks associated with virtual HR:

Cyber-Law Issue	No	Uncertain	Yes
1. Does your company have a legally sound e-mail policy?	1	2	3
2. Do you have a procedure for handling complaints about unauthorized or offensive on-line conduct by employees?	1	2	3
3. Are employees and developers routinely informed not to put any unauthorized copyrighted material on any company system? (Note: This includes not only text, but also pictures, video, and sound.)	1	2	3
4. Do employees sign agreements requiring them to use company computer equipment and software only for lawful business purposes?	1	2	3

Cyber-Law Issue	No	Uncertain	Yes
5. Are procedures in place to protect the confidentiality of all sensitive HR databases and on-line files?	1	2	3
6. Are effective password security systems and firewalls in place to control unauthorized access to HR information?	1	2	3
7. Do you effectively screen your information technology staff to prevent the negligent hiring of a potential thief or saboteur?	1	2	3
8. Does your corporate communications staff review all publications on your Web site to ensure that they are not misleading or fraudulent in their claims to employees and/or customers?	1	2	3
9. Do you make sure that all of your on-line recruiting, testing, and training practices comply with all professional and legal standards related to fair employment practices?	1	2	3
10. Is your computer equipment properly secured to avoid acts of vandalism?	1	2	3

Total Score =

Your score should range from 10 to 30. Use the follow guide to assess your commitment to reducing legal exposure related to virtual HR:

Score

10–16   *Low Commitment.* Take a course on how to increase your security and risk management practices in the area of information technology.

17–23   *Average Commitment.* You are at least committed to some forms of security management. Try to become more committed to developing a fail-safe risk-management system.

24–30   *High Commitment.* You are very committed to minimizing security risks that plague the Information Age.

7. DEVELOPING THE TECHNOLOGY-ENABLED ORGANIZATION

Corporations are experimenting with a wide variety of organizational designs that can benefit from the expertise of virtual HR professionals. In fact, these HR professionals must take the strategic lead in helping to design many organization structures. Some of the hottest organizational design fronts that need the virtual HR professional's immediate attention are listed below:

1. *Telecommuting*—This design involves employees who work at home and communicate with the office by electronic means. HR professionals need to design procedures to ensure safe and productive telecommuting experiences.

2. *Virtual Teaming*—Teams are the key to highly intelligent, flexible, and cost-effective organizations. Virtual teams are groups of complementary employees who are linked across time, space, and organizational boundaries with the aid of technologies such as Groupware and Intranets.

3. *The Portable Workplace*—Portability is essential for tomorrow's workplace. Virtual HR professionals need to design ways to let business technology travel everywhere with the employees.

4. *Virtual Corporate Universities*—Employees will be able to acquire job-relevant certifications and degrees on their corporate Intranet. Special lessons from leading instructors can also be hyperlinked to the virtual university's home pages. Corporations will be able to showcase the most knowledgeable instructors in the world.

5. *Virtual Corporations*—Many company's are focusing on their core competencies and joining with other organizations that bring complementary competencies to the mix. That is, virtual organizations can often find themselves in global networks with organizations that provide research, design, manufacturing, marketing, and support competencies. These virtual corporations are usually product and project focused. Hence, they are generally short-lived. Virtual HR professionals should be heavily involved in selecting partners and in documenting that all selected companies have the core competencies they profess to have.

Describe any technology-enabled work groups or organizations that you have helped to create at your company.

---

8. TURBOCHARGING YOUR CONTINUING EDUCATION

It is more important than ever for HR professionals to pursue an aggressive continuing education campaign. They should focus on applied information technology, strategic HR management, and contemporary business skills such as advanced project management.

HR professionals should pay special attention to the applied technology fronts. They should focus on emerging information technologies and how these technologies can cost-effectively facilitate and augment human resources management at their companies. The following initiatives should help:

1. *Learn by Doing!* Invest in a state-of-the art home computer system and master all available applications (e.g., word processing, spread sheets, database managers, presentation software, Internet access programs).

2. *Read, Read, Read!* Read computer dictionaries, software application manuals, and books on futuristic technology. Also read legal texts that cover such issues as on-line privacy protection and intellectual property law. Finally, when was the last time you read a contemporary book on strategic HR management?

3. *Get Trained.* Use off-the-shelf multimedia training software to quickly learn operating system and application software programs and suites. Attend training seminars that provide hands-on learning experiences. Try to learn the most job-relevant software packages first.

4. *Attend Association-Sponsored Training.* Many associations, such as the American Management Association, provide three-day seminars on topics such as strategic HR management and how to implement a well-designed information technology strategy for competitive advantage. Courses are also available for how to do business on the Internet, how to develop and implement corporate Intranets, and how to manage one's

time effectively while avoiding information overload. These types of seminars are highly recommended.

5. ***Go Back to School.*** I am a firm believer that if HR professionals want to excel in the 21st century, they should return to graduate school. They can take courses on corporate strategy and information technology. Some universities are even gearing their curriculum toward working professionals who are seeking contemporary degree programs. For example, the Keller Graduate School of Management offers niche graduate programs in human resources management, telecommunications management, and project management. Keller also offers coursework leading to a Techno-MBA; that is, one can take a set of core MBA courses along with a series of contemporary information technology courses. Virtual HR professionals can strengthen their career development program only by taking graduate-level courses that develop their strategic use of technology (see Scott, 1997).

Career Development Opportunities

1. What type of strategically-oriented HR classes would you currently benefit from?

_____

_____

_____

_____

2. Is there any information and technology management courses that would facilitate your career as a virtual HR professional?

_____

_____

_____

_____

3. What type of specialty courses (e.g., project management, business law, corporate communications) would increase your ability to implement and manage a virtual HR program?

_____

_____

_____

_____

PART 3

Review, References, Further Reading, and Appendices

Reading Review

____ ____ 1. Virtual HR is typically defined as the use of computer systems, interactive electronic media, and telecommunication networks and services to carry out the functions of the human resources department.

____ ____ 2. The primary goal of a virtual HR department is to reduce the administrative costs associated with the standard form of human resources management.

____ ____ 3. Intel's Pentium MMX processor chip is especially relevant to interactive multimedia software programs.

True False

——— ——— **4.** Client–server technologies deal with the integration of computers and telephones.

——— ——— **5.** On-line performance appraisals are the leading Web-based HR application.

——— ——— **6.** HR reengineering is typically defined as the fundamental rethinking and radical redesign of human resource processes to bring about dramatic improvements in overall productivity and service levels.

——— ——— **7.** Web browsers are compatible with most operating platforms.

——— ——— **8.** HR Web sites only need to receive thorough usability testing before they can be officially rolled out.

——— ——— **9.** A major Intranet blunder is going "Web crazy" by putting too much content on the Web that cannot be easily searched, accessed, and studied.

——— ——— **10.** Virtual career centers provide services to both job seekers and companies with job openings.

——— ——— **11.** Computerized personnel tests are no more accurate than computer-assisted interviews.

——— ——— **12.** Computer-based personnel tests are not required to comply with the same professional standards and employment laws that paper-and-pencil personnel tests must comply with.

True   False

_____   _____   13. The movement toward learning organizations and knowledge-competent workers is a major driver of computer-assisted training programs.

_____   _____   14. Distant-learning programs occur when employees participate in satellite- or Web-based training experiences at the exact same time as other trainees even though they are in different locations.

_____   _____   15. Virtual reality is too far out to have any practical utility in the workplace.

_____   _____   16. HR representatives can transform themselves into virtual HR professionals if they develop computer skills and master information technology.

_____   _____   17. Advances in information technology will threaten many HR jobs.

_____   _____   18. In the long run, it is better to develop all virtual HR programs and applications in-house.

_____   _____   19. Virtual HR professionals must increase their skills in the areas of strategic research and statistical analysis.

_____   _____   20. Virtual HR professionals must be available if any department wants to implement virtual teaming or telecommuting paradigms.

ANSWERS TO REVIEW QUESTIONS

1. **True**   Virtual HR professionals use computer hardware, software, and networks to carry out a wide variety of human resource management functions.

2. **False**   Another equally important goal of virtual HR is to improve a company's competitiveness and productivity.

3. **True**   The Intel MMX multimedia extension improves the performance of such tasks as the processing of graphics, video, and sound.

4. **False**   Computer telephony technologies deal with the integration of computers and telephones.

5. **False**   The leading Web-based application is virtual recruitment services (e.g., on-line job postings).

6. **True**   Virtual HR professionals always strive to utilize user-friendly technology that potentiates highly valid and reliable HR information.

7. **True**   Web browsers are compatible with nearly all platforms, and most employees are already familiar with Web browsing tools.

8. **False**   HR Web sites also need to undergo significant load testing to ensure that they can reliably handle the site traffic.

9. **True**   Virtual HR professionals should put only the most timely and critically important information on the Web.

10. **True**   Job seekers benefit from using searchable databases to identify companies with relevant job openings, while companies can

list both their domestic and overseas jobs on the virtual career center Web site.

11. **False**   While both types of assessment systems typically utilize cutting-edge item administration, scoring, and reporting software, a personnel test has routinely out-performed a set of interview items when it comes to predicting job performance accurately. This difference usually occurs because a test is more objective and standardized.

12. **False**   Computer-based tests have to comply with the same professional and legal standards that apply to traditional testing programs. (See Appendix B for a listing of such standards.)

13. **True**   Virtual HR managers are very committed to developing "intellectual capital" through information technology, including interactive multimedia and Web-based training programs.

14. **True**   In addition to satellite and Web-based training, desktop video-conferencing systems also support the distant-learning paradigm.

15. **False**   Virtual reality training modules are already being deployed in the workplace. Motorola is using VR training to teach employees how to run high-tech assembly lines. Surgeons also use VR training to practice very complicated surgery protocols.

16. **False**   It is true that aspiring virtual HR professionals must develop computer skills and master information technology. Yet they also need to develop contemporary work-related personality traits like team orientation, empowering others, managing chaos, self-management, and exhibiting a gold-collar work ethic. They also need to excel at strategic HR management.

17. **True**   The writing is already on the wall! However, by becoming more strategic and technologically literate and by developing a contemporary work-related personality, HR professionals will increase their chances of retaining their jobs within the reengineered HR departments.

18. **False**   The truth is that major aspects of the project should be outsourced unless your company's core competencies lie in developing and managing HR software applications.

19. **True**   Although this is a very demanding requirement, HR professionals must be able to transform HR data into strategically useful information quickly and accurately.

20. **False**   This approach is too passive and reactive. Instead, HR professionals must proactively identify opportunities for these new forms of technology-enabled organizational designs. The HR professional must also help to implement these new paradigms, especially since they will lead to strong competitive advantage.

References

Adams, Nina. 1996. "A Study of the Effectiveness of Using Virtual Reality to Orient Line Workers in a Manufacturing Environment." Master's thesis, DePaul University, Chicago, Illinois.

Asymetrix Corporation. 1997. *Distributed Training: The Opportunity for Training and Education*. Publication 1-17. Bellevue, Washington: Asymetrix.

Baisbridge, S. V. 1997. "The Implications of Technology-Assisted Training." *IHRIM.link*, December–January: 61–68.

Cahlin, M. 1997. "Search Engines: How to Find Anything You Want on the Web." *PC Novice* 5, no. 5: 189–191.

Callaway, E. 1996. "The Learning Web." *PC Week*, December 9: 53–57.

Callaway, E. 1997. "Avoiding Those Costly Intranet Blunders." *PC Week*, May 5: 137, 140.

Greengard, S. 1997. "Increase the Value of Your Intranet." *Workforce*, March: 88–94.

Hall, B. 1996. "Return on Investment and Multimedia Training." *New Media*, March 11: 23–24.

Jones, J. W. 1994. *Personnel Testing: A Manager's Guide*. Menlo Park, California: Crisp Publications.

Korzeniowski, P. 1997. "Intranet Bets Pay Off." *Infoworld*, January 13: 61–62.

Link, D. A. 1996. "HR on the Intranet." *IHRIM.link*, October–November: 36–44.

London House. 1997. *The Personnel Selection Inventory*. Rosemont, Illinois: London House Press.

Matlack, W. H. 1996. "How a successful Silicon Valley high-tech company maintains its competetive edge in recruiting people." HR/PC Quarterly, Winter Issue, Volume 12.2, no. 2: 4–6.

McNamara, P. 1997. "The Year of Videoconferencing is Here, Really!" *Network World*, May 5: 54.

Minneman, W. A. 1996. "Strategic Justification for an HRIS That Adds Value." *HR Magazine*, December: 35–38.

OmniTech Consulting Group. 1996. "Multimedia Training in the Fortune 1,000." *Training*, September: 53–60.

SAS Institute. 1995. *The SAS Data Warehouse: Supporting Creativity in Decision-making.* Cary, North Carolina: SAS Institute.

SAS Institute. 1997. *Data Mining with the SAS System: From Data to Business Advantage.* Cary, North Carolina: SAS Institute.

Schoenfeld, G. A. 1996. "Computerized Performance Appraisal: Product Reviews of Three Software Programs." *HR/PC Quarterly* 12, no. 1: 19–26.

Scott, K. 1997. "New Master's Program Weds Technology and Business Skills." *Network World,* April 28: 58.

Shadovitz, D. 1996. "Niche by Niche: Client/Server Isn't Necessarily the Last Word in the Migration from Centralized to Distributed HMS." *Human Resource Executive,* December: 35–36.

Stevens, L. 1997a. "Cases: Click Away." *Human Resource Executive,* March 6: 56–57.

Stevens, L. 1997b. "Cases: Global View." *Human Resource Executive,* March 6: 54.

Warek, G. M. 1997. "Training Software Implementation: Partnership for Success." *IHRIM.link,* December–January: 22–30.

Watson-Wyatt. 1997. "Empowering Employees: A Survey Report on Human Resources and the Web." (URL: http//www.watsonwyatt.com).

Wilder, C. 1997. "Big Insurer Offers Liability Coverage for Web Sites." *Information Week,* April 28: 67.

Further Reading

Bysinger, B., and K. Knights. 1996. *Investing in Information Technology.* New York: Van Nostrand Reinhold.

Calighain, T. 1997. *Netscape Guide to Internet Research.* Research Triangle Park, North Carolina: Ventana Communications Group.

Currid, C. 1994. *Reengineering Tool Kit: 15 Tools and Technologies for Reengineering Your Company.* Rocklin, California: Prima Publishing.

Currid, C. 1996. *Computing Strategies for Reengineering Your Organization.* Rocklin, California: Prima Publishing.

Freedman, A. 1996. *The Computer Desktop Encyclopedia.* New York: Amacom.

Gilster, P. 1997. *Digital Literacy.* New York: John Wiley & Sons, Inc.

Grenier, R., and G. Metes. 1995. *Going Virtual: Moving Your Organization into the 21st Century.* Upper Saddle River, New Jersey: Prentice-Hall.

Grochow, J. M. 1997. *Information Overload: Creating Value with New Information Systems Technology.* Upper Saddle River, New Jersey: Yourdon Press.

Jones, J. W., 1993. *High-Speed Management: Time-Based Strategies for Managers and Organizations.* San Francisco: Jossey-Bass Publishers.

Keen, P. 1997. *Business Multimedia Explained: A Manager's Guide to Key Terms and Concepts.* Boston, Massachusetts: Harvard Business School Press.

Lipnack, J. and J. Stamps. 1997. *Virtual Teams: Reaching Across Space, Time, and Organizations with Technology.* New York: John Wiley & Sons, Inc.

Lucas, H. C. 1995. *The T-form Organization: Using Technology to Design Organizations for the 21st Century.* San Francisco: Jossey-Bass Publishers.

Luftman, J. N. 1996. *Competing in the Information Age: Strategic Alignment in Practice.* New York: Oxford University Press.

Martin, J. 1996. *Cybercorp: The New Business Revolution.* New York: Amacom.

Shipley, C., and M. Fish. 1996. *How the World Wide Web Works.* Emeryvile, California: Ziff-Davis Press.

Appendix A

Virtual HR Lexicon

Virtual HR managers constantly strive to master the rapidly growing lexicon associated with the computer hardware and software technologies that are relevant to human resources management. The definitions of the following terms should be studied and understood if such professionals plan to interact in a credible manner with internal information technology staff, outside technology/content vendors, and senior executives.

Address—The location of a network computer or account. This includes the unique Internet protocol (IP) address by which each computer on the Internet is known to the other users.

America Online (AOL)—A leading commercial on-line service provider. AOL provides an appealing graphic user-interface, user friendliness, a clublike atmosphere, and Internet access, among other services.

Antivirus Program—Software that monitors a computer for viruses by isolating and reporting irregularities in a computer system.

Applet—A small niche application or utility, such as an organizational survey administration and scoring routine that performs just one useful task. The applet is designed for use within larger programs.

Application—An executable program capable of performing a specialized function such as word processing, spreadsheet analyses, and database management.

Audio Streaming—A software technology that allows sound files to be played on the Internet in real time, without the need to download them first.

Authentication—In networks, the procedure by which a computer verifies a user's identification. The most common forms of authentication include the utilization of a sign-on name and password protection to stored files.

Bandwidth—The amount of data that can be transferred simultaneously. All computing systems and data transmission paths (e.g., telephone lines) have a defined bandwidth, regulating the size of data packets that can pass through them.

Bit—The smallest unit of information in a digital computer: 1 or 0. Eight bits make up one byte. The number of bits used to record information, or used in one central processing unit (CPU) processing cycle, indicates the level of detail of the information, or the relative speed of the CPU. For example, an 8-bit CPU processes one-fourth as much information as a 32-bit CPU in each clock cycle.

Bookmarks—Commands that take users directly to World Wide Web pages that they visit frequently. Most commonly found in Web browsers and Internet organizers.

Broadcast—To transmit information to more than one person simultaneously. Computers allow us to broadcast text such as E-mail. Also known as "Webcasting" when information is broadcasted over the World Wide Web.

Browser—A software application that allows users to download, view, and print out World Wide Web pages and graphics on their own computers. Browsers allow employees to navigate from one Web page to the next with a mouse.

Bulletin Board System (BBS)—A computer system set up with one or more modems that serves as an information passage center that makes messages available for dial-up users.

Chat—Real-time communication over the Internet or an on-line service. This involves two or more people typing messages back and forth that appear on the other person's screen in real time.

Client—A computer used to make requests for data from a larger, more powerful computer.

Client–Server Networks—Networks allow clients to share information with each other. The network configuration includes, at a minimum, a database serving computer and one or more client computers. The server can be a personal computer, minicomputer, or mainframe, and it provides resources such as database management and distribution. Client computers download, process, and use data and information from the server.

Communication Satellite—An orbiting satellite used to relay signals from one point on the ground to another or between other satellites. Such satellites can handle large volumes of information.

Compact Disc Read-Only Memory (CD-ROM)—A computer data medium using compact disks to store digital data. A laser beam reads the CD-ROM.

Compression—A way of shrinking the size of computer files. Many large data files are packed in a compressed format to make them smaller. These files must be decompressed before they can be used.

Computer—A machine that accepts input, processes it according to specified rules, and produces output. A mainframe computer is a large, central computer with abundant memory, storage space, and processing capabilities that handle all the computations and storage for a group of input computers. A microcomputer is generally referred to as a desktop, or personal, computer. A minicomputer is a mid-sized machine that falls between mainframes and microcomputers in terms of power, size, and speed. Finally, both notebook and palm-top computers are designed to be very portable and to even run on batteries if necessary.

Computer-Aided Instruction—The use of software in teaching, including learning tools such as tutorials and tests. The interactive nature of these programs lets employees learn at an individual pace.

Computer-Based Training (CBT)—The use of computers to teach skills and assess learning retention. Most computer-based training programs use multimedia data sets.

Computer Conferencing—Computer conferencing is a feature of most large on-line networks. On-line sections of these electronic environments are created into virtual rooms, called "conference rooms" or "chat rooms." Computer users can gather in these "rooms" with other logged-on members of the network and chat with each other by typing lines of words.

Computer Crime—Any illegal or unauthorized use of a computer.

Computer Security—The protection of computers and the information contained in them from unauthorized access. Security also involves backing up all data and using passwords for access. Computer security prevents people from accessing, adding, removing, or altering files, causing data loss, or engaging in more serious computer crimes.

Connect Charge—The amount of money a user pays for connecting to a commercial communications service (e.g., an Internet service provider).

Connect Time—The period during which a user is signed on, usually for a fee, to an on-line service, bulletin board system, host computer, or Internet service provider.

Courseware—Educational or training software used in training facilities to teach employees about a specific topic.

Cross-Platform—The capability for hardware or software to run equally well on different platforms. For example, most Web browsers run on more than a dozen different types of computers.

Custom Software—A program developed to perform a specific task for a specific company, as compared with packaged, off-the-shelf software.

Cyberspace—Not a real location, but rather the "virtual world" occupied by one or more human beings, created and maintained by computers and related information technology. In this virtual space, people can do many of the things they do in physical space: interact with other people, read the news, attend training seminars, and even shop.

Database—A database is a collection of information that is divided into cross-referenced categories that can be flexibly manipulated, organized, and analyzed.

Database Management System—A program that arranges, secures, and retrieves the information in a computerized database.

Data Encryption—The transcription of data into an indecipherable code for security purposes. Encrypted data is incomprehensible until it has been converted back into its original form.

Data Mining—Statistically analyzing a large database in order to find strategically important relationships among the data.

Data Warehousing—A method of storing, managing, and cataloging very large relational databases on a computer with sufficient memory and processing power.

Digital—Modern computers are digital because they use the fixed binary digits 0 and 1 to represent all data. Digitizing is the process of converting linear pictorial images and sound into digital data for storage. For example, a sound card can digitize a sound by translating it from analog (its actual sound) to digital (a form that can be read by a computer). Scanners also convert nondigital images such as photographs and text into a digital format.

Download—To retrieve an application or file from another computer through a network connection or modem.

Electronic Mail (E-mail)—Text messages sent through a network to a specified individual or group. E-mail can be delivered within seconds or minutes across thousands of miles.

Enterprise-Wide Network—A network that connects computers throughout an organization, including those in different buildings, cities, states, or even countries. This type of network includes computers, servers, gateways, and other components.

Extranet—Extranets use the common format of the World Wide Web to link companies, their customers, and suppliers to a private network. These diverse groups can exchange data electronically rather than sending paper-based information back and forth.

Fax—The transmission of graphics or text across telephone lines. Faxes are typically sent and received from fax machines. However, the trend is to use fax/modems, which can digitize the information from an application such as a word processor and send it to any fax machine or fax/modem on any type of computer.

Fax-on-Demand—With fax-on-demand software and a fax/modem, a company can set up a system in which callers use Touch-Tone phones to request faxes on a wide variety of topics offered by the company.

File Server—A file storage device on a local area network that is accessible to all users on the network.

File Transfer Protocol (FTP)—A widely used transmission control protocol/Internet protocol for transferring text or binary data files from one computer to another. Internet users may use FTP applications to log in to FTP servers and download files.

Firewall—Software or hardware that limits certain kinds of access to a computer from a network or other outside source.

Forum—An area on an on-line service or bulletin board system where people with a common interest can post messages to one another. Forums are frequently used to share information or debate ideas.

Graphical User Interface (GUI)—A GUI, pronounced "gooey," is a graphics-based interface that lets you access programs by pointing to icons, buttons, and windows rather than typing a string of commands at a command prompt.

Groupware—A category of software that runs primarily on client–server networks and Intranets. It allows users to share information via electronic messaging and other on-line information-sharing protocols. Groupware typically includes database management and document-sharing capabilities, too.

Handshake—This friendly phrase describes what two modems do when they connect with each other.

Home Office—Dedicated office set up in the home, usually with financial support from the employer. The employee is not assigned corporate office space.

Home Page—The name for the main page in a Web site where users can find hyperlinks to other pages in the site.

Hyperlink—An icon, graphic, or word in a file that, when selected with a mouse, automatically opens another file for viewing. World Wide Web pages often include hyperlinks that display other Web pages when clicked on by the user.

Hypermedia—Electronic media containing links to other sections, works, or media, allowing instant cross-referencing.

Hypertext Markup Language (HTML)—The basic language used to build hypertext documents on the World Wide Web.

Hypertext Transfer Protocol (HTTP)—The text-based protocol that serves as the official language of the World Wide Web. This protocol defines high-level commands and methods that Web browsers use to communicate with Web servers.

Integrated Services Digital Network (ISDN)—A digital telephone network that transmits data in digital form (1s and 0s) rather than analog form. ISDN is a fast and convenient way to access the Internet.

Integrated Software—Software consisting of several applications specifically designed to work together. For example, an integrated software package might include a word processor, a spreadsheet, and a database.

Interactive Video—A video-intensive computer program that lets users control or influence the way the video is played. Interactive video is most often found in training simulations.

Internet—A computer network linking millions of computers for communications purposes. Commercial industries, corporations, and home users all communicate over the Internet. The Internet is often accessed through commercial on-line services (e.g., America Online).

Internet Service Provider (ISP)—An organization that lets users dial into its computers to connect to its Internet link for a fee. These providers supply not only an Internet connection, but also e-mail addresses and World Wide Web browsing software.

Intranet—The corporate equivalent of the World Wide Web. Companies can store HR forms and documents on their Intranet Web sites that reside safely in a private network. Employees can easily find HR information on their company's Intranet by using standard Web browsers.

Java—A very promising programming language from Sun Microsystems, Inc. Java makes it easier to create programs that are written once and then can run on nearly any computer or platform. Java inspired the development of applets, tiny application programs that can be electronically downloaded to PCs or other devices as needed.

Keyword—Keywords are used with on-line search engines to locate related information. When you want to locate files relating to a particular subject or a program whose exact name you have forgotten, searching with the help of keywords is a useful feature.

Legacy—A reference to the technology associated with old corporate computers and systems.

Local Area Network (LAN)—A group of computers, usually in one building, that are physically connected in a manner that lets them communicate and interact with each other. For a LAN to operate, it needs a server, which is a computer that holds data used by the different computers on the network. Local area networks allow users to share document files and expensive equipment such as laser printers.

Local Area Wireless Network—A network that uses radio transmissions instead of cables to connect computers.

Microsoft Network—A commercial on-line network. Access to the service comes bundled with the Microsoft Windows 95 operating system.

Modem—Modems allow a computer to transmit and receive data and information over telephone lines. Modems convert analog data into digital data that computers can read, as well as convert digital data into analog data so it can be transmitted back over the telephone lines.

Multimedia—Typically, a computer-based presentation that blends text, graphics, audio, video, and animation from various sources into an integrated application.

Multitasking—The process of having a computer perform multiple tasks simultaneously.

Netiquette—A term for on-line etiquette. Nettiquette establishes the basic expectations for proper conduct on the Internet.

Netscape Navigator—Currently, one of the most widely used Web browsers on the Internet.

Network—A set of electronically connected computers that can share storage devices, peripherals, and applications. In-house wiring, telephone lines, cable connections, and satellites can be used to connect computer networks.

Network Administrator—An individual responsible for the maintenance and operation of a computer network.

Network Architecture—The most basic unifying structure of hardware and software that ties a group of interconnected computers together. Well-designed architectures ensure quality communication and data transfer.

Network Computer—Network computers are streamlined and stripped-down computers that are ideally designed for use with the Internet. This class of computers is often referred to as simple "electronic appliances." Network computers are connected to the Internet and can do many tasks associated with more powerful personal computers, but for a fraction of the cost.

On-line—A reference to interacting on Intranets, the Internet, or commercial on-line services.

Open System—In communications, a network designed to incorporate devices from any manufacturer, as long as the device can use the same communication protocols and facilities. When applied to specific hardware or software, an open system is one that accepts add-ons from third-party suppliers.

Operating System—An operating system is the basic internal software that runs a personal computer. It is the operating system that determines basic aspects of a computer's procedures, such as how files are named and stored, how the disk drives are accessed, and how the user will interact with the computer on the monitor.

Optical Scanner—An input device that renders an image or text as a digital image. This image then can be converted into a text-based or graphics file using optical character recognition (OCR) software. Material that has been scanned into the computer can be edited, faxed, sent by E-mail, and printed.

Paperless Office—The idea of creating and storing all office information and documentation in computers, eliminating the need for paper.

Password Protection—A system that protects a computer or files from unauthorized users.

Platform—A collection of technology and software that companies use in developing and/or delivering their products and services. This word also has other meanings in the field of information technology. For example, a platform can be a chip, a computer, an operating system, an application, a network, or any combination of these.

Plug and Play—The ability of a computer to detect and configure a new piece of hardware automatically, without the user having to reconfigure hardware elements physically.

Programmer—A person who writes the codes that make up a software program. (Note: The current trend is to refer to programmers as developers.)

Programming Language—A language that allows programmers to communicate their instructions to a computer. Assemblers, compilers, and interpreters turn the programmer's language into the machine code that a computer can understand. Some examples of common programming languages include BASIC, COBOL, C++, Java, and Visual Basic.

Relational Database—A database that can share information across multiple tables or files. These tables can be linked by common information. A major advantage of relational databases is that the same information can exist in multiple files simultaneously.

Search Engine—The software that searches a database for information specified by the user. Search engines are used in many virtual HR applications such as Internet research, resume management software, and on-line job searches, to name a few.

Server—A midrange computer that stores files, databases, and programs used by other machines, or clients.

Site License—A license that gives permission to use a software package on more than one system legally.

Software—A set of coded instructions that tell a computer how to process data.

Telecommunications—Transmitting data electronically over a communications line. Telecommunications include using a modem to send a file, using a fax machine to send a document to another person, and using a modem to access an on-line service.

Telecommuting—To work at home and communicate with an office via telecommunication lines.

Teleconference—A teleconference (also known simply as a conference or an on-line conference) is any conversation held in real time and conducted over telephone lines.

Telephony—Technology that lets users employ a PC to make and receive telephone calls. Telephony software often includes features such as auto dialing, onscreen messaging, and voice mail.

Traffic—The amount of activity that is taking place on a communications system such as a corporate Intranet.

Transmission Control Protocol/Internet Protocol (TCP/IP)—A collection of networking protocols that are "the glue that binds the Internet." For example, TCP/IP allows disjoint, dissimilar, and spatially separated physical networks to be joined together to form one large virtual network, or Internet.

Universal Resource Locator (URL)—A standardized naming or addressing system for documents and media accessible over the Internet. Often referred to as the "phone number" or "address" for World Wide Web sites.

User-Friendly—The attribute of a software program or computer system that means it can be learned and used with relative ease.

Videoconferencing—A conference among participants situated at different sites on a computer network that are connected by video cameras, microphones, and a messaging system. Attendees each sit in front of a camera and microphone, and view and listen to the other participants as information is transmitted through the network to a computer screen and speakers.

Video Streaming—A software technology that allows video files to be played on the Internet in real time.

Virtual—Something that exists in essence or effect without a physical presence. The word "virtual" connotes something that is not what it appears to be. Virtual reality, for example, is made up of computer-generated images and sound.

Virtual HR—A form of human resources management that relies on cutting-edge information technologies to carry out a few or many of the functions in HR. Originally, virtual HR was implemented as an efficiency program. It is now seen as being a major source of competitive advantage.

Virtual Reality—The sense of place and being that exists in cyberspace. An artificial, computer-generated environment in which users interact with the environment and objects in it through specialized input devices such as goggles, headphones, and gloves. Three-dimensional images, moving sound, and tactile feedback provided by the special input devices create realistic situations when generated by high-end computer systems.

Virtual Reality Modeling Language (VRML)—The three-dimensional counterpart to HTML, VRML is a scriptlike language that permits rich three-dimensional scenes to be described in simple text files and displayed in VRML-capable Web browsers.

Voice Mail—A computer-based telephone answering system in which callers choose options that help them reach the voice mailbox of a particular person, and then offers options for how a message is recorded and delivered.

Voice Recognition—A computer's ability to recognize spoken words and act on them as if they were keyboard or mouse commands. Voice recognition is typically used in situations where users' hands are either too busy or otherwise unable to operate a keyboard or mouse.

Web Browser—Software that provides access to and navigation around the World Wide Web. Browsers allow users to download Web pages at different sites either by clicking on hyperlinks (i.e., graphics or text that are presented in a different color than the rest of a document and that contain programming code which connect to another page) or by entering a Web page's address or universal resource locator.

Web Master—A person responsible for the day-to-day management and maintenance of a Web site.

Web Page—A document written in Hypertext Markup Language (HTML) that can be accessed on the Internet. Web pages can contain information, graphics, and hyperlinks to other Web pages and files. Web pages are found by addresses, or universal resource locators.

Web Site—A World Wide Web location that provides information such as text, graphics, and audio files to users as well as connections (called hypertext links, hyperlinks, or links) to other Web sites on the Internet.

Wide Area Network (WAN)—A collection of computers connected to each other over a wide geographic area. Wide area networks usually require special arrangements with telephone companies because data is transmitted among locations across telephone lines.

Workstation—Personal computing system optimized for high performance. Typically, workstations include high-performance, high-resolution graphic display systems and use the UNIX operating system. Workstations are typically considered to be more powerful than PCs, but that difference is fading quickly.

World Wide Web (WWW)—A graphic interface for the Internet that is composed of Internet servers which provide access to documents that in turn provide hyperlinks to other documents, multimedia fields, and sites. These links are different-colored text or graphics that contain programming code which provides the actual connection to another Web site.

APPENDIX B

Professional and Legal Standards

Virtual HR professionals strive at all times to use only valid and reliable assessment content that meet all state and federal legislation. That is, these professionals know the importance of using scientifically and legally sound assessment instruments that can be delivered through their enabling technologies. The following professional standards and employment legislation should, therefore, be adhered to at all times.

STANDARDS

1. American Educational Research Association, American Psychological Association, and National Council on Measurement in Education. 1985. *Standards for Educational and Psychological Testing.* Washington, D.C.: American Psychological Association.

2. Society for Industrial and Organizational Psychology, Inc., American Psychological Association. 1987. *Principles for the Validation and Use of Personnel Selection Procedures,* Third Edition. Arlington Heights, Illinois: Society for Industrial and Organizational Psychology.

3. American Council on Education. 1995. *Guidelines for Computerized-Adaptive Test Development and Use in Education.* Washington, D.C.: American Council on Education.

4. Equal Employment Opportunity Commission, Civil Service Commission, Department of Labor and Department of Justice. 1978. *Adoption of Uniform Guidelines on Professional Selection Procedures. Federal Register,* 43 (166): 38290–313.

NEWER LEGISLATION

1. *The Americans with Disabilities Act of 1990 (ADA):* The Americans with Disabilities Act of 1990 is one of the most significant pieces of legislation affecting individuals with disabilities that has ever been enacted. The ADA is designed to eliminate discrimination against individuals with disabilities in a variety of critical areas including employment, public and private services, transportation, communication, and recreation. The ADA makes it unlawful to discriminate against a qualified individual with a disability in employment settings. Under the ADA, a person has a disability if he or she has a substantial physical or mental impairment or a record of such an impairment. A substantial impairment is one that significantly limits or restricts a major life activity such as hearing, seeing, speaking, breathing, performing manual tasks, walking, caring for oneself, or learning.

The ADA makes it unlawful to discriminate with any type of virtual HR practice, including selection, recruitment, promotion, training, dismissal, compensation, job assignments, leave, and benefits. Still, an individual with a disability must be qualified to perform the essential functions of the job with or without reasonable accommodation. The applicant must also satisfy a company's job requirements for educational background, employment experience, skills, licenses, and any other qualification standards that are job-related.

2. ***The Civil Rights Act of 1991:*** The Civil Rights Act of 1991 prohibits the use of any personnel assessment systems that employ different norms or cutoff scores based on race, color, religion, sex, or national origin. This act makes it an unlawful employment practice for an employer, in connection with the selection or referral of applicants or candidates for employment or promotion, to adjust the scores of, use different cutoff scores for, or otherwise alter the results of employment-related assessment systems on the basis of race, color, religion, sex, or national origin. This law requires that an individual's assessment scores be accurately recorded without adjustment or alteration and that a single cutoff score be applicable to all persons, regardless of protected group status.

3. ***State Privacy Laws:*** A few states have enacted privacy protection laws that are more extensive than those at the federal level. These state laws and labor codes define and protect privacy for government employees and in some cases for the private sector. For example, in some states private-sector employees have the right to access, review, and file for amendment of their personnel records. All information collected about private-sector employees must be necessary and properly used for specific job-related purposes. Hence, companies should use virtual HR applications that meet a definite business need instead of applications that were not originally developed for the workplace.

About the Author

John W. Jones, Ph.D., ABPP, is senior vice president of research and technology at NCS/London House, Rosemont, Illinois. London House is a human resources consulting firm that specializes in computer-based assessments for business and industry. Dr. Jones is also the founder of the Business Psychology Research Institute, Arlington Heights, Illinois. The institute is the sponsor of the *Journal of Business and Psychology,* a scholarly periodical devoted to articles on all aspects of psychology that apply to business settings.

Dr. Jones is the senior editor for *Applying Psychology in Business: The Handbook for Managers and Human Resource Professionals* (Lexington Books, 1991). He also wrote *Preemployment Honesty Testing: Current Research and Future Directions* (Quorum, 1991), along with *High-Speed Management: Time-Based Strategies for Managers and Organizations* (Jossey-Bass, 1993). His most recent book is *Personnel Testing: A Manager's Guide* (Crisp Publications, 1994). Dr. Jones has published over 100 articles and frequently presents his research at scholarly, professional, and trade conferences.

Dr. Jones is a member of the American Psychological Association, the American Psychological Society, the Society for Industrial-Organizational Psychology, and the Society of Psychologists in Management. He is also a member of the Society for Human Resources Management and the International Association for Human Resource Information Management. Dr. Jones is also the Chair of the Association of Test Publisher's Testing Standards Committee.

Dr. Jones holds a B.A. in psychology from the University of Cincinnati; an M.A. in applied experimental psychology from DePaul University, Chicago; and a Ph.D. in psychology, specializing in industrial-organizational psychology, applied research, and counseling psychology, also from DePaul University. Dr. Jones was awarded the Diplomate in Industrial-Organizational Psychology by the American Board of Professional Psychology. He is also a licensed psychologist in Illinois. Dr. Jones is completing his MBA in strategic marketing from Keller Graduate School of Management, Chicago, Illinois.

Finally, Dr. Jones is the editor of the *Virtual HR Professional,* a quarterly newsletter dedicated to the education and development of HR managers and professionals for the 21st century. For subscription and fee information, you can reach Dr. Jones at:

Dr. John W. Jones
Business Psychology Research Institute
824 East Rand Road, Suite 274
Arlington Heights, IL 60004
Phone: 847-292-3380
Fax: 847-255-3480
e-mail: BPRI2000@aol.com